JUVENILE
IN JUSTICE

Juvenile courts in the U.S. annually process an estimated 1.7 million cases of youth charged with a delinquency offense — approximately 4,600 delinquency cases per day.

On any given day, approximately 70,000 young people are in juvenile detention or correctional facilities each night.

America's heavy reliance on juvenile incarceration is unique among the world's developed nations.

The cost for a typical stay in a juvenile detention facility is $66,000 to $88,000 to incarcerate a young person for 9 to 12 months.

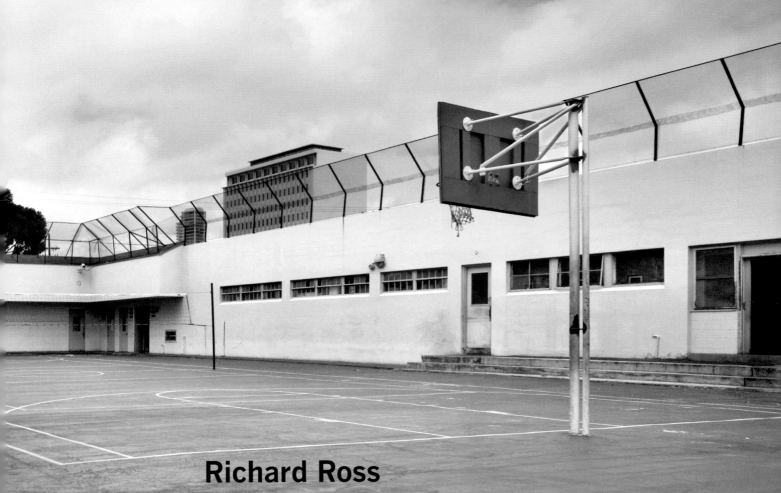

Richard Ross
JUVENILE
IN JUSTICE

Photographs and Afterword © 2012 Richard Ross
Foreword © 2012 Ira Glass
Preface © 2012 Bart Lubow

Support for this project has been provided by The Annie E. Casey Foundation.

For more information, to read the blog, get updates, and find out how you can take action and get involved, see the website **www.juvenile-in-justice.com**

Juvenile in Justice may be purchased for educational, business, or sales promotional use. For information, please write: Richard Ross, 142 Santa Rosa Place, Santa Barbara, CA 93109, or email: rross@richardross.net

Design and editorial and production management: Laura Lindgren, New York
Copyediting and proofreading: Don Kennison

FRONT COVER: A 12-year-old juvenile in his windowless cell at Harrison County Juvenile Detention Center in Biloxi, Mississippi, operated by Mississippi Security Services, a private company. There is currently a lawsuit against MSS that forced it to reduce the center's population. An 8:1 inmate to staff ratio must now be maintained.

BACK COVER: At Mendota Juvenile Treatment Center in Wisconsin, the cells have a trap in the door for security and for meals. Before this boy can be released from his cell, he has to put his hands through the slot for shackling.

TITLE PAGE: No one has visited me here. No one. I'm not here for a status violation. They got me charged with more than that. I talk to the judge tomorrow. I have to touch the wall for doing what they call "antisocial" behavior—only a "procedure violation," nothing big. I've been touching the wall for a while now. Doesn't matter what part of the wall I touch as long as I have some part of me on the wall. I am trying to get some sleep here. —J.B., age 17. Hale Ho'omalu Juvenile Hall, Honolulu, Hawaii, built in the 1950s, is now closed; detainees occupy a new facility.

CONTENTS: Three girls dance while other girls (unpictured) drum on the tables. There are 113 girls in this facility. PO said a lot of these girls are gang members and are really tough. Central Juvenile Hall, Los Angeles, California.

ISBN: 978-0-9855106-0-2

Printed and bound in China through Asia-Pacific Offset

10 9 8 7 6 5 4 3 2 1

SUPERIOR COURT OF CALIFORNIA
COUNTY OF LOS ANGELES

30

IN THE MATTER OF:_____

A MINOR

DEPT.	DATE	CHRONOLOGICAL INDEX OF COURT PROCEEDINGS

CONFIDENTIAL

CONFIDENTIAL

CONTENTS

FOREWORD by Ira Glass

Years ago I interviewed this 15-year-old named Jacqueline Montanez, who made herself famous among Chicago gangbangers one night in 1992 when she and two other girls lured two boys into the public bathrooms in Humboldt Park, promising to mess around. Jacki kissed one of them on the mouth, pulled out a gun, and shot him in the back of the head. She handed the gun to another girl who shot his friend.

Bad, right? That's a girl who's different from every 15-year-old you've ever met, right?

But talking to Jacki was like talking to any teenager. I know that's not a profound insight. What else would she be? But before I sat down with her, I didn't know what to expect. Most of us have so little contact with kids who commit serious crimes, me included. I pictured a sullen sociopath, a teen murderer like in an old film. Writing these words I realize how stupid that was.

The reality was that Jacki was a show-off, with a lot of anger and a drive to dominate certain situations. And the murders — horrible as they were — had a logic to them. They were revenge killings, gang retaliation, Jacki proving her toughness. In short, she seemed normal. In conversation, in the course of a minute, she'd swerve from bragging to cracking a joke to confession, like so many kids that age I've interviewed. A typical quote:

> We [girls] wanna show off too. We wanna let 'em know, the guys ain't
> the best, the girls can do better. 'Cause we try to be bigger than guys.
> So we walk like guys and we're tough like guys. Some of us even look
> like guys!

A 15-year-old girl on suicide watch, under constant surveillance. In this behavior unit the residents become extremely jumpy and verbal when any event breaks their routine. At the moment all the girls are in their cells. In the entire facility, approximately 75 percent of the population have mental health needs, and of these, 67 percent take psychotropic medication.

The construction paper names on the wall celebrate the corrections officers that work the unit. Macon Youth Development Campus, Macon, Georgia

That's a joke, that last line. Then Jacki explained that the girls in her crew wouldn't wear skirts or makeup.

> You know, we're too tough to wear makeup. Usually we're in our jogging clothes and our gym shoes ready to fight. I had to just be a stud. I'd walk with my hand between my legs like I had something there to grab. And a lot of guys would be like "You're so attractive but why you are acting like a boy?"
>
> I be like, "If you don't like it, just step."
>
> And then when they see me go into a bar with miniskirts and makeup and heels and stuff, it's like "Look at her!" They really freak out. They freak out.

Here her voice on the tape gets kind of dreamy. It still made her happy to think about it.

> And it used to feel good. Because one day I'll be a boy and the next day I'll be a girl.

See what I mean? She'd gone through some messed-up things in her life, but she was also doing the normal teenaged "I'll dress this way and see how it feels" kinds of tinkering around that anyone does while figuring out who they are.

I thought about Jacki when I looked through the pictures in this book. The kids all look so vulnerable. So normal. It's hard to get your head around the fact that these are the criminals, that these are the kids who need locking up. There's no way around this word—they look so innocent. Because they're so young. The fact that we never see their faces in these photos (for legal reasons, because they're minors) makes the effect even more intense. The lack of specific facial details, I found, eliminated anything that might keep me from imagining them as my teenaged nephews and nieces or their friends.

And what do you call the look—the visual aesthetics—of the jails and prisons we put them in? Going into these places reporting various stories, I've learned that usually they're not squalid places. This isn't Dickens; they're not dank and awful in the way you'd fear. Often they're bright, modern, squeaky-clean. Painted in cheerful yellows and blues and oranges. Witness the time-out chair on page 82, which would not be out of place in a grade school classroom, with its crooked construction-paper sign declaring that this is the "SETTLING AREA." It's the sterility of these spaces—the bare, freshly painted concrete walls, the unadorned floors—that makes the truth of what they're for so obvious and makes them seem so impersonal. These are cages. And like any cages they're probably very lonely places to live in. Looking through this book, sometimes I get the sense that someone went out of his or her way to design a space that would be humane and livable for these children, but you can't get around the fact that a prison cell is a prison cell is a prison cell. It's going to make you feel bad. It's built into the premise.

> You can't get around the fact that a prison cell is a prison cell is a prison cell.

Richard Ross has managed to take very expressive pictures of these very unexpressive places. It's obvious this book is a labor of love.

I get why he wanted to do it. These kids are mostly invisible. These lockups are places that few of us ever enter. And if you do enter the gates and pass through the first barbed-wire-topped fence and the second one, after you're searched and you wait awhile on some plastic chair to be let deeper inside the facility, when you finally see how the prisoners live, it can be unsettling. I get the same feeling I get sometimes walking into a stranger's house. It's the opposite of impersonal. I see their stuff. I see too much.

And yes, we all know that under current juvenile offender laws, way more teenagers are behind bars than in the past. But seeing it for yourself is different. There's something about the literalness of "Oh, this is where they live." "This is what it looks like." I'm not sure if I can articulate why that's so powerful. I guess it's as dumb and straightforward as: it turns the abstract idea of juvenile justice into something as real as a bed, a T-shirt, a toilet. It becomes possible to imagine what it would be to be one of those kids. And once you start imagining that, who knows where it can lead?

"What percentage of girls have been sexually abused when they come here?"

"What percentage? Every one. All 88 girls in our custody."

Dr. Les Forman, director, Maryvale Residential Program, Rosemead, California

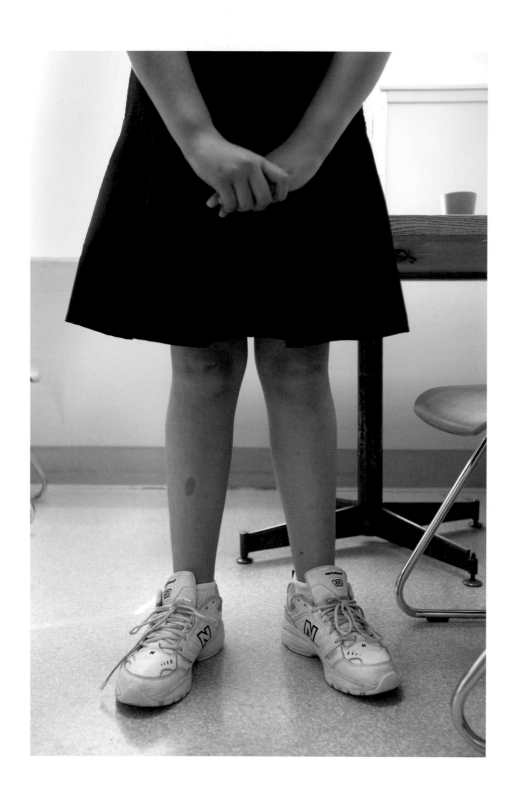

PREFACE by Bart Lubow

Richard Ross's pictures in this book expose, with unprecedented breadth and detail, some of the most opaque facilities in our country. The oral documentaries in Ira Glass's *This American Life* are perhaps the most insightful, revealing, and entertaining portraits of our society available on radio and a regular highlight of my weekends.

So, given my admiration for both of these people, initially I was confused by parts of their commentaries for *Juvenile in Justice*. To provide one example, Ross, in his afterword, cites a visit with a young man who is being prosecuted as an adult for multiple, violent charges. Glass, to provide another example, begins his essay with a 15-year-old girl who murdered someone essentially for fun. Both of these case studies significantly distort the offense profile of the typical teenager in juvenile corrections facilities. Although these extreme examples may help "hook" readers in order to make larger points about these kids and these institutions, the ways that individual or anecdotal stories can reinforce inaccurate generalizations or false stereotypes alarm juvenile justice reformers such as myself.

In trying to reconcile some of the dissonance created by our varied perspectives, I began to appreciate that we bring different lenses to a project like this and that, perhaps, multiple lenses are needed to fully understand the subject. Put another way, the three of us approached this issue from different angles and through different mediums but all with the same ultimate concern—the juvenile in trouble. Richard Ross evidently thought enough of this insight to invite me to share some thoughts on the juvenile jails and prisons depicted here from the perspective of someone whose 40-year career has been devoted to minimizing the use of these awful places.

What's wrong with juvenile detention and corrections facilities? Many of Ross's pictures provide poignant evidence for the reader. What the photos can't provide, however, are the aggregate trends, general facts, and historical truths behind the individual snapshots. Here's what people like me understand about these places.

A young girl at Maryvale, an all-girls level-12 institution in Rosemead, California

Juvenile detention and youth corrections centers are commonly dangerous and abusive. Over the past 40 years, 80 percent of U.S. states have operated juvenile institutions whose conditions were so violent, dirty, restrictive, and bereft of basic services that either a federal court intervened or a major scandal erupted. Lest the casual reader think that these constitutional and moral deficiencies are a relic of the past, the majority of these patterns of persistent maltreatment were revealed only since 2000. This means either that administrators haven't learned from past problems or — more likely — that environments like these are simply toxic by nature.

Juvenile corrections facilities can look relatively benign, even in some of these pictures and especially when compared to infamous adult prisons such as Attica or San Quentin. But years of investigations, research, and litigation reveal the truth. Kids in these places are commonly subjected to physical abuse and excessive use of force by staff. According to the Associated Press, for example, 13,000 claims of abuse were reported from 2004 through 2007. In 2010 the federal government released a report on sexual abuse that found 12 percent of youth (1 out of 8!) in juvenile facilities had been victimized during the prior year by staff or other youth. Far too frequently, confined youth are physically or chemically (e.g., mace) restrained and isolated in their cells (typically called "rooms" in juvenile justice parlance, a dialect prone to euphemism) for lengthy periods without legal recourse. Staff, too, it must be acknowledged, are assaulted and injured with disturbing frequency.

These institutions are often unnecessary and generally ineffective. People commonly assume that the youth confined in facilities such as those in this book are all gangbanging, gun-toting thugs who pose uncontrollable public safety risks. But only about 12 percent of the nearly 150,000 annual admissions into residential facilities by juvenile courts are for the FBI's "violent index offenses." In many states, as many as half of the kids in confinement are youth committed for misdemeanors. Youth are more likely to be in these places for property offenses, violations of court orders, and low-level drug charges than they are for acts of interpersonal violence.

Why do we incarcerate youth who pose relatively low risks to public safety? There are many explanations, including the system's often well-intended but misguided search for "services"; counterproductive financial incentives that encourage commitments to state custody; and our society's historical tendency to punish defiant teenage behavior. What's most important to realize, however, is that the rate of juvenile confinement in the United States is neither inevitable nor necessary. U.S. youth incarceration rates are approximately 18 times greater than France and 7 times greater than Great Britain, despite only marginal differences in youth offending rates.

All this unnecessary incarceration is even more distressing when we examine long-term outcomes. Multiple recidivism studies reveal that youth discharged from corrections facilities are rarely rehabilitated or deterred from future criminal behavior. For example, in states that measure recidivism 3 years after discharge, about three-quarters of formerly confined youth are arrested for a new offense. Many studies indicate that incarceration is no more effective than probation or alternative sanctions in reducing future criminality; others suggest that correctional placements exacerbate criminality. Incarceration is especially ineffective for less serious offenders, whose risk of future criminal behavior increases as a consequence of confinement in these facilities.

> **Those confined are youth without voices, from families without resources, in communities without power.**

Taxpayer dollars are wasted on these retributive responses to delinquency.
The institutions in Ross's pictures are ridiculously expensive to operate. According to the American Correctional Association, it costs, on average, $88,000 per year to incarcerate a single youth in a juvenile correctional facility. By comparison, a four-year public university costs less than $8,000 per year.

The high cost of confinement has important consequences: it distorts the juvenile justice budget so that the lion's share of public dollars is devoted to a relatively small percentage of the overall court caseload. Investments in delinquency prevention or early intervention programs are effectively precluded because so many dollars are required to support the system's "deep end." This phenomenon is especially disturbing considering what we have learned over the past couple of decades as to what works to combat juvenile crime. "Evidence-based programs," for example, have been rigorously tested and repeatedly shown to produce better long-term results than juvenile confinement, yet investments in these programs remain limited because public dollars continue to go predominantly down the incarceration drain.

A fundamental question arises: if these places are so dangerous, so ineffective, so costly, why do we persist in these practices? Again, there are many answers, including politicians' tendency to pander in public safety matters and the compelling economic interests associated with a $5 billion annual industry. But certainly one of the key explanations for the public's lack of perspective on these troubling institutions is who is locked up: overwhelmingly youth of color from the most disadvantaged neighborhoods in this country. Those confined are youth without voices, from families without resources, in communities without power. Indeed, the extreme racial and ethnic disproportionality in patterns of confinement, especially when considered in light of these institutions' awful track records, raises another fundamental question of whether this system would persist if its wards were white, middle-class youth.

The good news is that the tide seems to be turning. Over the past decade, in multiple states in all parts of the country, we have seen dramatic reductions in youth incarceration. These changes have occurred for different reasons in different places, but collectively they add up to a national de-institutionalization trend. In a recent report, researchers documented that more than 50 juvenile institutions had been shuttered in 18 states between 2007 and 2011. Equally important, these significant reductions in youth incarceration did not undermine public safety. In fact, those states with the largest decreases in confinement experienced the greatest decreases in youth crime.

Right now, these trends are the sum of idiosyncratic developments in individual states, rather than a reflection of a clear national policy consensus that juvenile incarceration should be used far more sparingly, only for the relatively few extremely dangerous youth. But that consensus can't be far off. Sustained low rates of juvenile crime, tight fiscal times for state and local governments, growing knowledge about what works, and a national detention reform movement collectively provide a perfect storm of conditions that can push American juvenile justice policy and practice beyond its unhealthy reliance on incarceration. Hopefully, this book's photographic documentation will add to this movement by increasing public awareness of those places where the system punishes and isolates misbehaving youth.

Bart Lubow, Director, Juvenile Justice Strategy Group
The Annie E. Casey Foundation, Baltimore, Maryland

L.T., first time in custody, age 15, King County Youth Service Center, Seattle, Washington

I went to day school next door to this place for eight months. When I went back to regular school I got in a fight in three days. A kid was calling my mom bad names. I punched him and left school and started beating up a car. Cops came for me and I wouldn't put on my seat belt when they put me in their car. So that was another violation. I told them I didn't want to come back here…but here I am. I've been here a week and have a week to go. I'm "sanctioned" for two weeks. —N.R., age 12

Douglas County Juvenile Detention, Lawrence, Kansas

I've been here like 4 days or a week. Sometimes I like being in my cell or watching TV or eating lunch or making Christmas decorations. I'm here because of something I did with my brother. He's like 19 or 24, I don't know. I'm in sixth grade. I live with my mom and dad. My brother is arrested right now. They just had me out of my school. He was arrested for aggravated robbery from a Quik Mart. I'm in special ed in school. I can hardly spell but I can read some. I was ditching school a lot. My mom and dad have visited me twice. They're both on SS. I'm in lockdown for "improper behavior." —C.P., age 12

Pima County Juvenile Detention Center, Tucson, Arizona

ABOVE: I lived with my mother until I was 5. No idea who my father is. I got kicked out of my grandma's house. She took me in just to get money from the government. She threw me out because I have an African American boyfriend and we have 2 kids, one 4 months and the other 16 months, and she couldn't take it any more. I got an IUD implant so I won't get pregnant again for at least 5 years. I have 10 siblings. We all live around the islands but never have been raised together and never see each other. I was 84 pounds when I came here. Now I am up to 98. Yeah, meth. —K.T., age 17

Coysa Shelter, Haleiwa, Hawaii

OPPOSITE: I got kicked out of school for partying and truancy. I use meth. They have had me here for 2 weeks. I think they keep me here because they think I am a risk of hurting myself. When they want to come in, they come in, they don't knock or anything—this is the observation room. There are 5 other girls here I think for things like runaway and curfew violations, lewd and lascivious conduct, trafficking meth, burglary, marijuana, molestation abuse, stuff like that. —C.T., age 15

Southwest Idaho Juvenile Detention Center, Caldwell, Idaho

Nearly 3 of every 4 youth confined in a residential facility for delinquency are not in for a serious violent felony crime.

I'm waiting for my mom to come get me. Is she in there? She's at work today. I want to go home. I got in trouble at school today. —R.T., age 10

Washoe County Detention Facility, Reno, Nevada

R.T. was brought in from school by a policeman. He stabbed a schoolmate, but it is unclear what the tool was, a pencil, knife, fork... He was waiting to be picked up by his mom, who couldn't come get him until she got off work for fear of losing her job. He was checked on every 5 minutes. The director of the facility recalled an 8-year-old being brought in for taking a bagel and stated, "This is not the place for these offenses."

I was gang-raped. The pictures were sent around on one of the guys' phone. The pictures got to all my friends and family. I've been here 3 days on a PV. We do arts and crafts with the littler boys. —K.B., age 15

Pima County Juvenile Detention Center, Tucson, Arizona

RIGHT: I'm from Philly. I've been here 14 months. My parents put me here because they had 5 "Amber" alerts for me. I ran away a lot with my boyfriend, who was 26. I'm adopted. I was sexually abused when I was younger. I think it costs my parents $9,000 a month to keep me here. —J.R., age 18

Cross Creek Program, Residential Treatment Center, La Verkin, Utah

BELOW: Interview room with anatomically correct dolls at Sexual Assault Response Team (SART) facilities, Santa Barbara, California

I was brought here by transporters. They took me out of my house in the
middle of the night and next thing I knew I was here. Been here 13 days. I have
to wear this red jumpsuit because I'm a "flight risk." I'm from San Jose. I live
with my mother, stepdad, and 3 sisters. I don't get along with my stepdad. I'm
a sophomore in high school. Basically, at home I smoke weed, hate school,
and just focus a lot on my music. I play guitar—any and every genre. I wasn't
skipping school. My mother doesn't know me very well. My parents are
divorced. I'm more like my dad—something my mom doesn't like so I just don't
listen to her—she goes against me all the time. My mother hasn't written me.
I am just doing my work. All I want to do is get out of here. —P.C., age 15

Red Cliff Ascent, Wilderness Treatment Program, Springville, Utah

Research shows that youth confined for longer periods of correctional confinement are no less likely to reoffend than youth confined for shorter periods.

I was 13 years old with my boyfriend. We were both extremely high. We were burglarizing a house in the high desert. The owners came in…and the crime escalated. I've been in this cell since I was 14. I have been sharing this cell with another woman ever since. I think it's 7 x 10. I've been eligible for parole, but on 4 different occasions the families of the victims were present to speak against my release. If it was my family, I would do the same, but I am a different person at 20 than the drugged child I was at 13. Now I'm the head of a women's firefighting unit that works with locals and assists in brush clearing, mud slides, and forest fires. I'm due for release in 4 years and 3 months. I age out of the system. They have to let me go when I turn 25. — C.H., age 20

Ventura Youth Correctional Facility, Camarillo, California

I've been here awhile. I have a 10-month-old baby that I would like to see, but that ain't gonna happen soon. I get to see the baby every Thursday. His daddy is in prison waiting to be sentenced for attempted murder. —J.K., age 17

Horizons Juvenile Center, Bronx, New York

J.K. was referred to in news reports as "Queen of the Bloods" and has been charged with killing and dismembering 2 people.

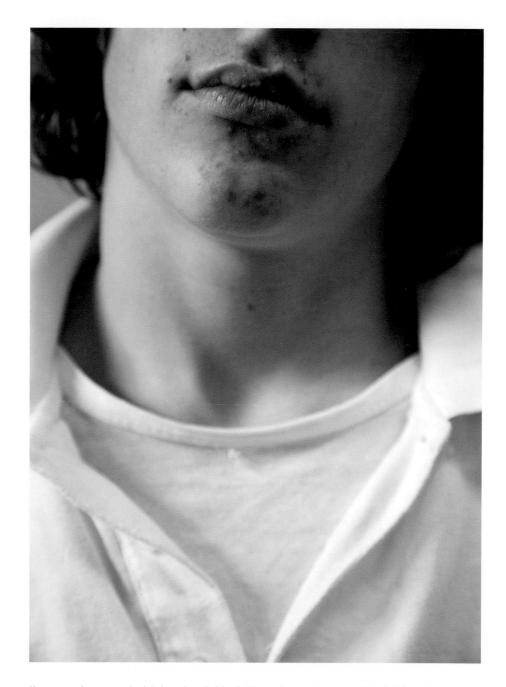

I'm a sophomore in high school. My father abused me, and he told me he was going to do the same to my little brother and sister. When he told me he was going to hurt them...I couldn't let that happen. He was asleep, so I took his gun and shot him. I pled guilty to a manslaughter plea. I had just turned 14 when it happened. My brother and sister can't visit. I miss them a lot. I am Christian and go to church every Saturday. I don't like showing my emotions. I would rather keep things neutral. If I let my emotions get into it...control can all fall away. Being able to control, this is my real strength. —Z., age 16

Juvenile Corrections Center, Nampa, Idaho

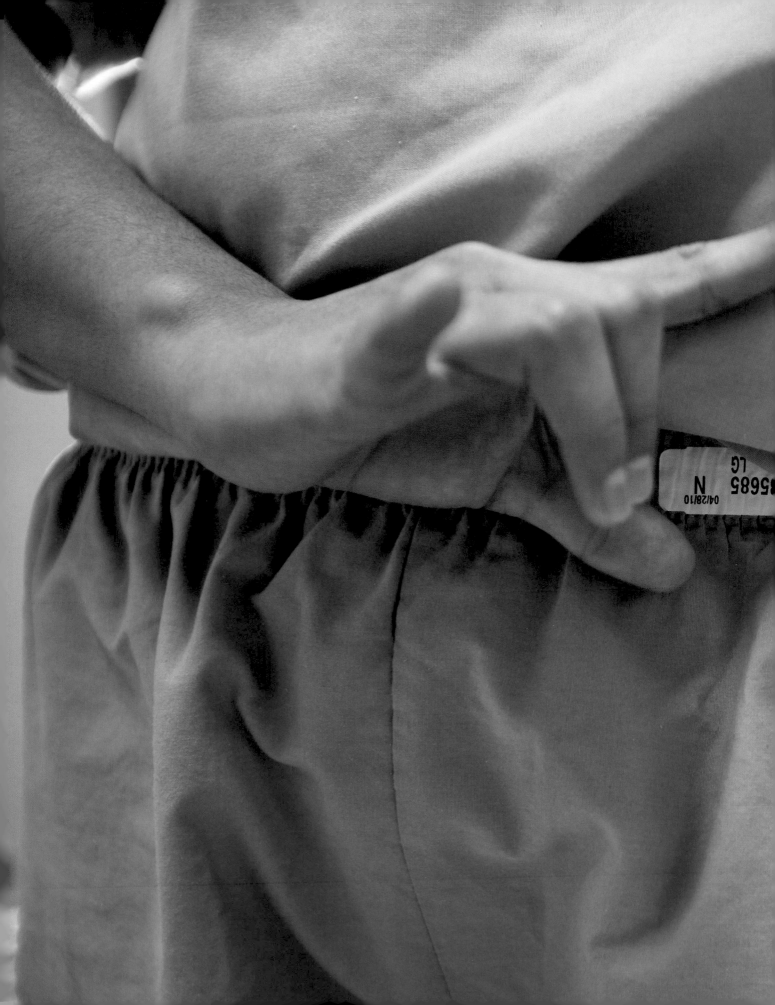

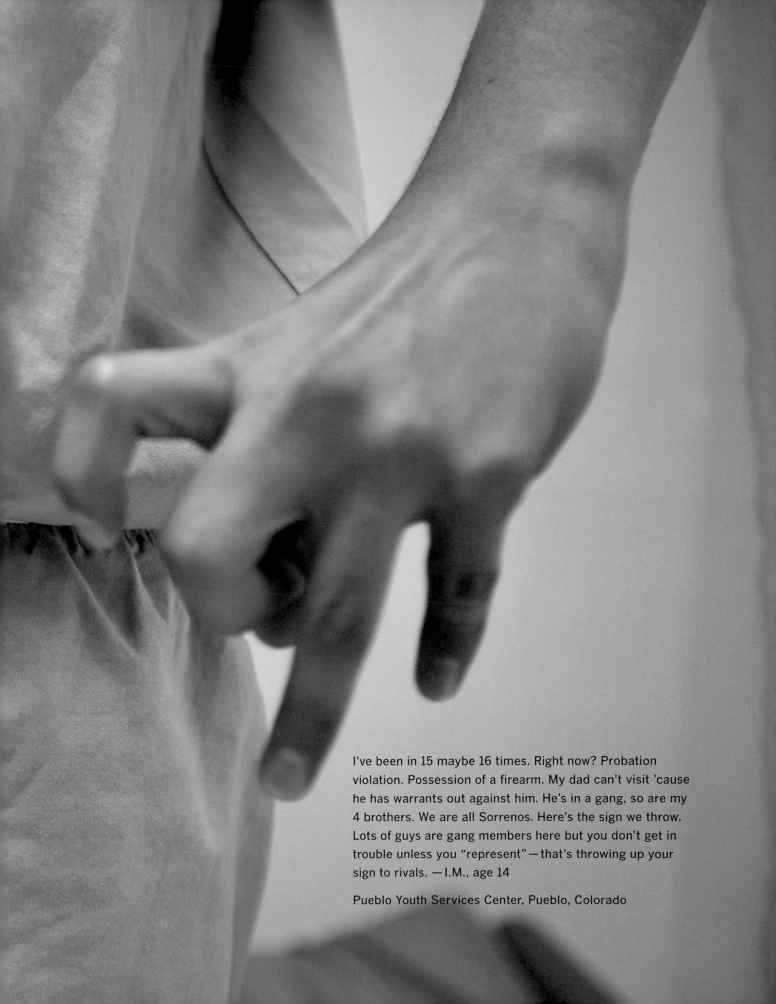

I've been in 15 maybe 16 times. Right now? Probation violation. Possession of a firearm. My dad can't visit 'cause he has warrants out against him. He's in a gang, so are my 4 brothers. We are all Sorrenos. Here's the sign we throw. Lots of guys are gang members here but you don't get in trouble unless you "represent"—that's throwing up your sign to rivals. —I.M., age 14

Pueblo Youth Services Center, Pueblo, Colorado

In September 2010 Grant County, Wisconsin, authorities accused a 6-year-old boy of first-degree sexual assault of a child for allegedly playing "doctor" with a 5-year-old girl.

I've been here for a week. I think they call this the observation room. I go to class in the morning and then comes back to my room. I don't like to read and there is no TV to watch. I sort of sit here, eat here — you know. I was supposed to come home today, but my aunt didn't come. I can't live with my mom or dad. I've been here 3 times before. This is the longest. My aunt doesn't visit...she never sure when the visiting days are. Actually I didn't tell my aunt that I'm here [she has to be notified]. —G.P., age 14

Southwest Idaho Juvenile Detention Center, Caldwell, Idaho

G.P. is "low functional," as described by the detention head, who tells me that Child Protective Services is involved as well. G.P. has very slow mannered speech. He has been charged with battery against his aunt. The striped suits, which are standard issue here, have been banned in other states as early as 1904 for being "too dehumanizing."

I was with a group of guys when I was 13. We jumped this guy near the lake. We got about $400. They gave me the gun 'cause I was the youngest. I been in Juno cottage for 2 years. I was coming back from the med unit with a homie and we broke into the canteen through a window and ate all the candy bars we could find. He got sick and we only had a 5-minute pass so they caught us. I got sent to Valis but got played by a staff there so they sent me here to Martin. —S.T., age 15

Ethan Allen School, Wales, Wisconsin

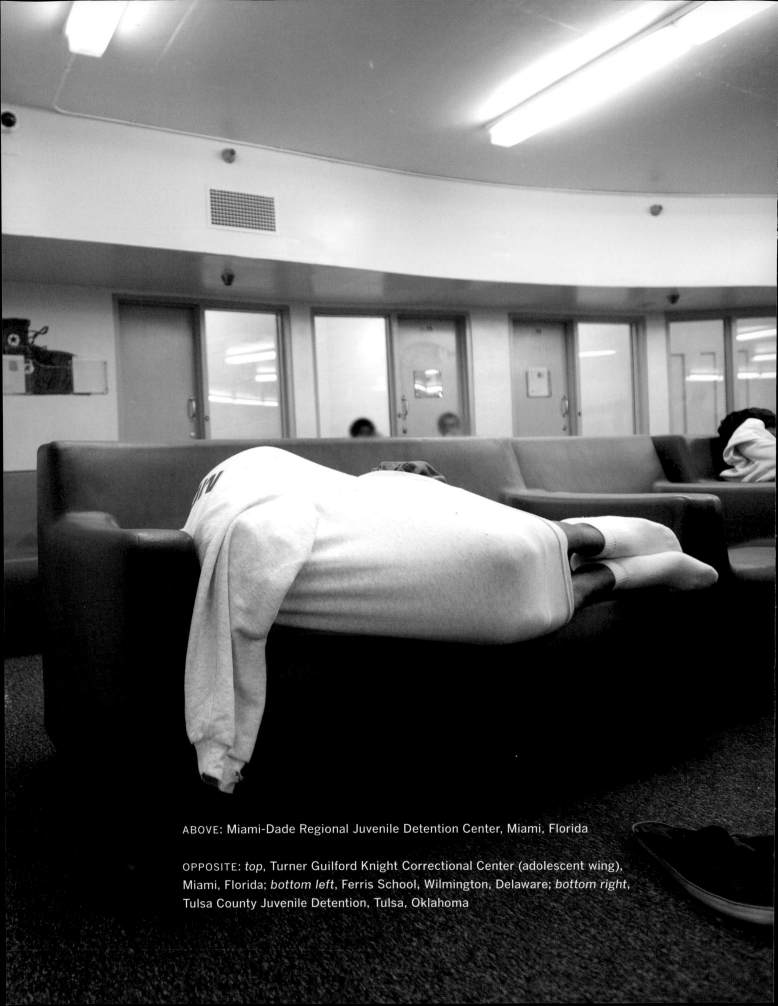

ABOVE: Miami-Dade Regional Juvenile Detention Center, Miami, Florida

OPPOSITE: *top*, Turner Guilford Knight Correctional Center (adolescent wing), Miami, Florida; *bottom left*, Ferris School, Wilmington, Delaware; *bottom right*, Tulsa County Juvenile Detention, Tulsa, Oklahoma

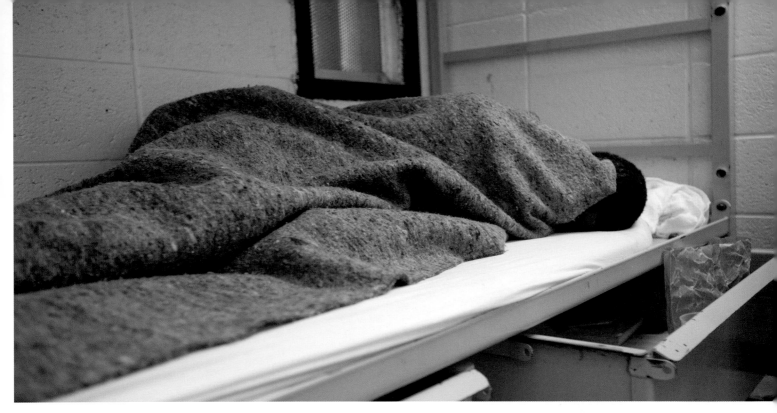

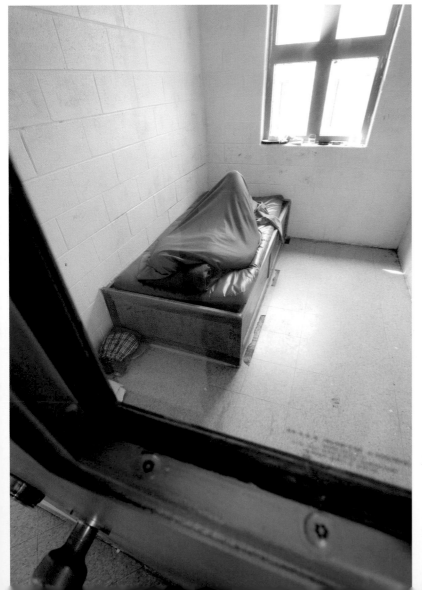

Programs offering counseling and treatment typically reduce recidivism, while those focused on coercion and control tend to produce negative or null effects.

A staff member conducts pat-down searches on juveniles at Miami-Dade Regional Juvenile Detention Center, Miami, Florida.

ABOVE: Lookout Mountain Youth Services Center in Golden, Colorado

OPPOSITE: They come in once a day and do a search of my room. Everything I have in there, *everything*, goes out — including the inside of the mattress and a body search — once a day. It happens any time. Random. I was arrested for assault against a 13-year-old girl. It's sort of all right, but it also really sucks. You have to listen to officers and do exactly what they tell you to do. I'm the only girl in here, so it's boring and lonely. I'm here for VOP [violation of probation]. I was at home with an ankle bracelet but ran away to Juárez with my boyfriend and another couple. They got married in Juárez. I got mad at my mother and started throwing chairs and cut my ankle bracelet. I've been here 4 months now. —D.M., age 14

Challenge Program, Juvenile Detention Facility, El Paso, Texas

Juveniles in the Challenge Program sit in their cells
at the Juvenile Detention Facility, El Paso, Texas.

Orientation Training Phase (OTP), part of the Youth Offender System (YOS) Facility in Pueblo, Colorado. OTP performs intake and assessment of convicted kids and is set up to run like a boot camp, with staff yelling at kids all the time. All of the kids at OTP have juvenile sentences with adult sentences hanging, meaning that if they mess up, they will have to serve their adult sentence. For example, a juvenile could be there serving a 2-year juvenile sentence with 15 years hanging.

Except in cases where juvenile offenders pose a clear and present danger to society, removing troubled young people from their homes is expensive and often unnecessary — with results no better (and often far worse) on average than community-based supervision and treatment.

(Left) I'm 16, in for aggravated assault.

(Right) I'm 12, from Milford. They're just holding me here temporarily. They should be moving me in a day or two.

Roommates. NFI Lakeside Assessment, Peabody, Massachusetts

(Left) I'm from Newburgh. It's a tough town, right near here. I think I was first charged when I was 9. I was a robbery lookout. I got caught in a big raid they did in town. I'm still in elementary school. — L.R., age 11

(Right) Yeah, I'm a Blood — live in Harlem. I been here 1½ months. Should get out in 2. I was transferred here from Lincoln. — S.T., age 16

Juvenile Treatment Center, Red Hook, New York

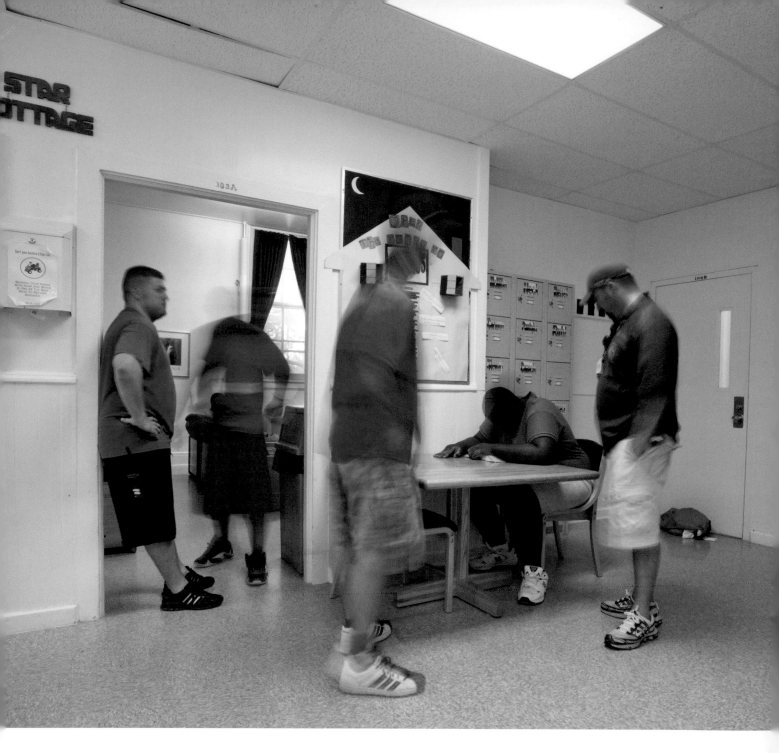

Don't touch me. Don't touch me. Don't touch me. Don't touch me. Don't touch me. Don't touch me. Don't touch me. Don't touch me... —D.R., age 17

Loysville Youth Development Center, Loysville, Pennsylvania

K.Y., a 15-year-old Filipino/Japanese boy [in the cell, not shown] in the mental health wing of the Alternatives to Secure Detention, is under 24-hour observation and checked on every 15 minutes. K.Y. didn't leave his house or attend school for 3 years. He assaulted his mother when she was brushing her teeth because she didn't clean his room quickly enough. His mother doesn't want him and placement will be difficult. The first step will be reconciliation with his mother.

King County Youth Service Center, Seattle, Washington

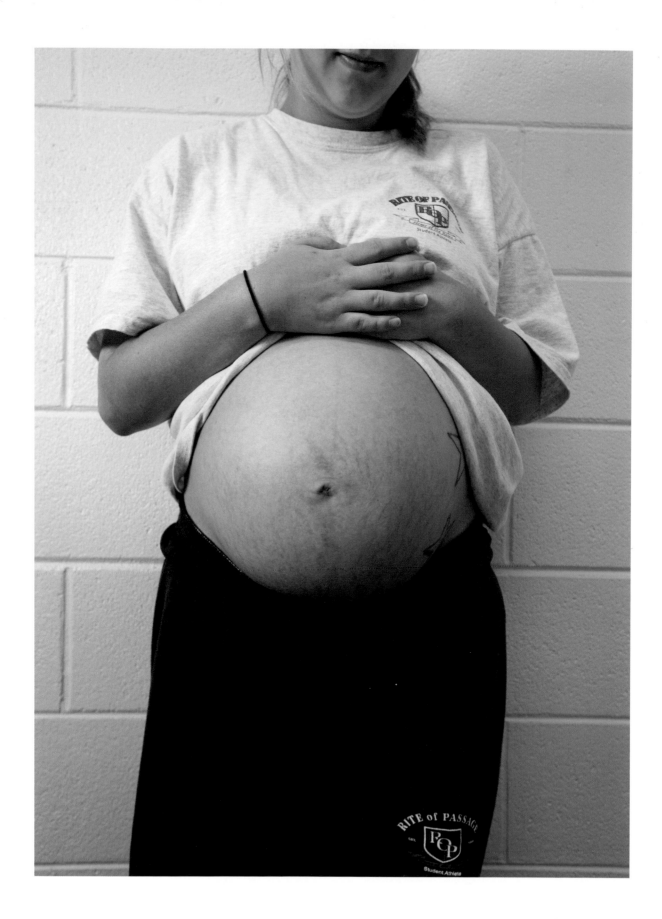

ABOVE: Model of a nursery made by residents at Maryvale, a level-12 lockdown institution in Rosemead, California

OPPOSITE: My boyfriend and I decided to get pregnant, but he left. We were together for 7 years. I was on community placement and back and forth for parole violations. Once I get out of here I owe the county 108 days for running away. I'm going to name the baby Addison. —A.G., age 19

Betty K. Marler Youth Child Care Center, Denver, Colorado

I have a 2½-year-old son and a 4½-month-old daughter [pictured]. I've been here 25 days. My mom brings my kids for me to visit. This is my first time here. I was under house arrest and then I violated parole by leaving the state. My parents are divorced. I had a bad UA [urine analysis] on parole. I did really bad at school. My mom, she had to quit her job working in construction to take care of my kids. She's in her late thirties. We couldn't get treatment for me in Minnesota...they wouldn't recognize my problems until they were way out of control. So now here I am in North Dakota. —S.S., age 17

North Dakota Youth Correction Center, Bismarck, North Dakota

Model of a cell at Ventura Youth Correctional Facility, Camarillo, California, made by a 17-year-old female inmate over 2 days.

Two-thirds of males and three-quarters of females in the juvenile justice system meet the criteria for one or more psychiatric disorders.

ABOVE: Alameda County Juvenile Detention Center, San Leandro, California, has a capacity of 360 kids, was built at a cost of $135 million, and opened in 2007, LEED Gold Certified. Oleoresin capsicum pepper spray is used in the building.

OPPOSITE: Protective equipment for staff in the event of extreme behavioral disorders/ outbursts. Mendota Juvenile Treatment Center, Wisconsin

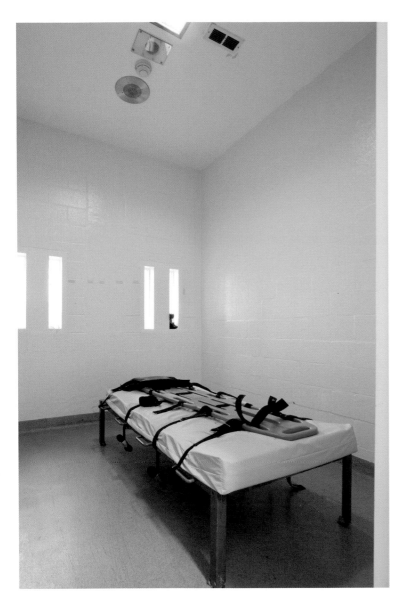 

Various forms of restraint, at 4 facilities. LEFT: MacLaren Youth Correctional Facility, Woodburn, Oregon; RIGHT: Washoe County Detention Facility, Reno, Nevada

LEFT: Mendota Juvenile Treatment Center, Wisconsin, where a male juvenile bit a vein in his arm and was restrained, at which point he began to chew off the insides of his cheeks and spit out the residue in a deliberate exhibit of control and will, and when released from the chair he pulled his teeth out; RIGHT: North Dakota Youth Correction Center in Bismarck, North Dakota

ABOVE: Crisis room, Kapolei, Oahu, Hawaii, a new facility about to be opened, with a capacity projected at 66

OPPOSITE: A settling chair, where unruly juveniles are sent to calm down and rethink their behavior, used in place of a confinement cell. Elliot Assessment, Pod A, part of Paul T. Leahy Center, Worcester, Massachusetts

Youth housed in adult jails are 36 times more likely to commit suicide than youth housed in juvenile detention facilities.

ABOVE: I'm on suicide watch—told them I was going to hang it up. I'm from the projects in the Bronx. I've been in and out of the system since I was 12. My original charge was possession of a weapon. I'm a straight-A student, in the eleventh grade. Nobody visits me here, no phone calls, no letters. I was raised by my grandparents, but all 3 died of strokes in the last 3 years. One of my sisters owns half of Ralph Lauren, the other is a physician—they're 22 and 24. My family wanted me to become a cop. I despise cops. I am waiting sentencing. I might get 24 months. —D.R., age 16

Bridges Juvenile Center (Spofford), Bronx, New York, a secure detention facility built in 1957 with a maximum capacity of 75 kids, closed March 2011

OPPOSITE: I was first arrested when I was 10, of battery against a teacher. I was also arrested for DUI, indecent solicitation of a minor, and breaking and entering. I'm a Blood of sorts, but my dad is a Crip. He has 12 kids living with him. My mom has 3 kids. Both my mom and dad are half black, half white. They have me wearing this suicide tunic the first 24 hours I am in here or longer, depending. I've been here before, done this before, worn this before. —O.P., age 15

Douglas County Juvenile Detention, Lawrence, Kansas

B.P., age 18, is self-abusive, not taking his meds, combative, and won't think twice about hurting staff. He is being held in the crisis intervention unit, on 24-hour supervision. He is wearing only his underwear. Half the staff is female, and thus they will supervise a male, although they don't watch him shower or use the bathroom. His clothes are removed when he goes in the unit to prevent him from hanging himself.

MacLaren Youth Correctional Facility, Woodburn, Oregon

Camera monitoring of the isolation room at St. Louis
Detention Center, St. Louis, Missouri

ABOVE: Observation room at Hawaii Youth Correctional Facility (HYCF), Kailua, Hawaii, built for 56 kids but presently housing 72. An annual $14 million is spent on HYCF, mostly on staff and poor management of overtime and contracts. Most of the kids here have come from horrific situations of abuse and/or drugs and addiction.

OPPOSITE: Security camera in an isolation cell at Ventura Youth Correctional Facility, Camarillo, California

ABOVE: A female juvenile with scars from cutting herself that read "Fuck Me"

Washoe County Detention Facility, Reno, Nevada

OPPOSITE: Suicide prevention practice dummy, Fairbanks, Alaska. Here the dummy demonstrates the taking of one's life by hanging with a bedsheet from a desk drawer.

Despite the pervasiveness of substance abuse, 42 percent of youth residing in juvenile corrections facilities do not receive any substance abuse treatment.

I'm from Riverside originally. I was living in Las Vegas, partying a lot, doing lots of drugs, and trying to be a DJ. They tried to guilt trip me into living with my grandmother. She runs a bunch of women's shelters. My mom is emotionally distant and my stepdad is really aggressive. They are Catholic and Jehovah's Witnesses and don't like that I am gay. I am here for curfew violation and running away from rehab. I do X, acid, MDMA, and I drink. I shouldn't be in rehab, as I stop doing drugs whenever I want. I am not addicted to anything, I just take different drugs when I want.

Being gay in a place like this is hell. A lot of guys think they can have sex with me anytime they want because they are in prison so it doesn't make them gay. And it doesn't count as long as they are giving rather than getting. These are a bunch of closet fags and a lot of homophobics. If I report them to the staff they hate me. I am here for 4 to 6 months...but I am not sure I will make it. —A.W., age 16

Nevada Youth Training Center, Elko, Nevada

I am a transgender female. They have me living in an isolation area for the past 7 months I think to protect me against suicide, but also keep me sort of away from the other girls. I live on the street with older friends who are part of "that life." They're mostly people who are positive about who I am but also got involved in stuff like burglary, drugs, and prostitution. I don't mind being separate from the other girls, but I miss the interaction. —A.S., age 17

Hawaii Youth Correctional Facility (HYCF), Kailua, Hawaii

I've been here 3 days. I was charged with running away from a group home.
And also larceny and 7 more runaway charges. I took my mom's car and then
tried to evade police. So I got an assault. My dad lives with my stepmom — both
are heavy drinkers. My dad is a construction worker. My stepmom takes all my
dad's attention. She's an accountant. My mother gave up custody of me last
year. She is schizo, bipolar with psychotic tendencies. She works at a hospital.
The eye? I got into a fight with my girlfriend. She punched me so hard I went
flying across the room and got a road rash on my shoulder. My eye looks a
lot better now. I got hit 2 weeks ago. My girlfriend is a big track and volleyball
player. She hit me because I used to have drug and alcohol problems. I said I
would stop drinking, but I came into her house drunk. She lives with our best
friend, E. She was living with her family, but they moved away and left her. I
hope E's mother will adopt me or at least be my guardian. Before this incident
I got Bs and Cs in school. It is pretty difficult being gay and Christian in a land
of homophobes. Actually it's pretty impossible here. —A.B., age 14

Tulsa County Juvenile Detention Center, Oklahoma

I got into a fight with a Blood. I didn't get hurt in the fight, but when they put me in solitary I punched the wall and broke my hand in 3 places. My trial is tomorrow. I think the charges for menacing will be dropped but I don't know for sure. I got in a fight with a guy that was hassling my mom. No one called me from home or visited me here yet. —R.G., age 15

Bridges Juvenile Center (Spofford), Bronx, New York, a secure detention facility built in 1957 with a maximum capacity of 75 kids, closed March 2011

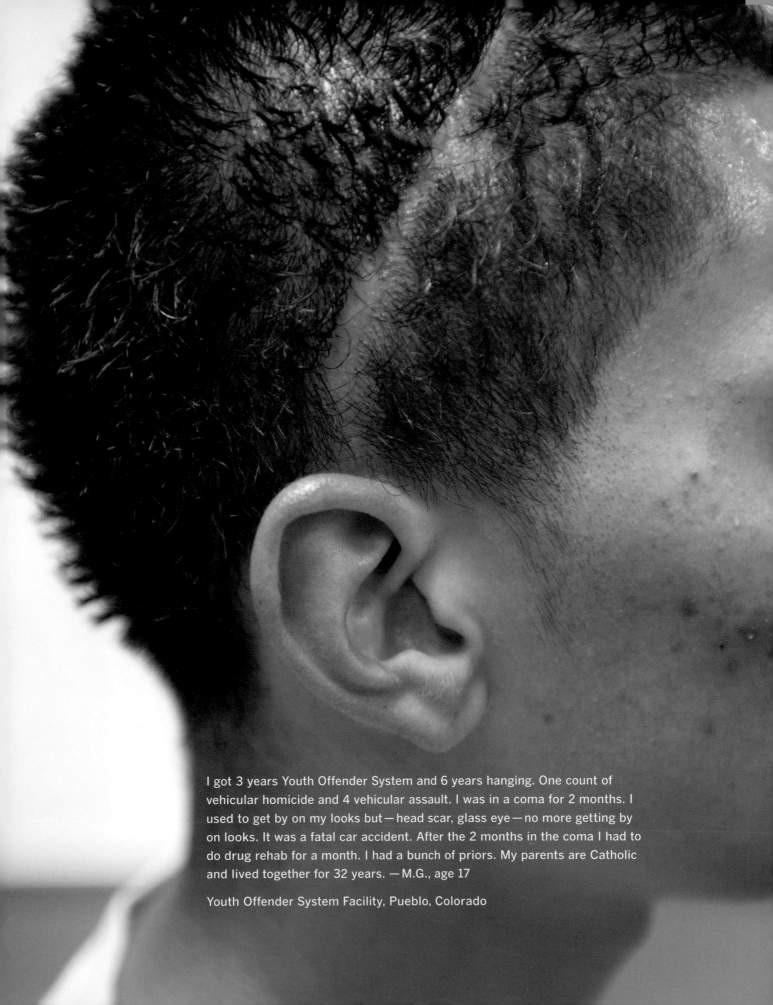

I got 3 years Youth Offender System and 6 years hanging. One count of vehicular homicide and 4 vehicular assault. I was in a coma for 2 months. I used to get by on my looks but — head scar, glass eye — no more getting by on looks. It was a fatal car accident. After the 2 months in the coma I had to do drug rehab for a month. I had a bunch of priors. My parents are Catholic and lived together for 32 years. —M.G., age 17

Youth Offender System Facility, Pueblo, Colorado

RESTRICTED ACCESS
ONLY AUTHORIZED VEHICLES DELIVERIES
PERMITTED BEYOND THIS POINT

INSIDE FENCED AREA, DO NOT LEAVE
VEHICLE RUNNING AND UNATTENDED SHUT
OFF ENGINE, REMOVE KEYS & LOCK UP

FOR DELIVERIES:
• IF UNSURE OF DESTINATION USE
  CALL BOX TO ASK FOR DIRECTIONS
• HAVE AN AUTHORIZATION OR
  PURCHASE ORDER NUMBER READY
• VEHICLES ARE SUBJECT TO SEARCH
  UPON ARRIVAL AND DEPARTURE

Ethan Allen School, Wales, Wisconsin

Intake at Los Padrinos Juvenile Hall, Downey, California

California's juvenile system "is broken almost everywhere you look." Deficiencies include "high levels of violence and fear...frequent lockdowns...and capitulation to gang culture."

I was picked up for probation violation. I'm not happy being here…even less happy having to stay here. I just met with some people from the court, CPS, and probation, I think. They told me I "turned the corner." —B.R., age 14

St. Louis Detention, Missouri

When a juvenile is brought in, a meeting is held with a court officer, Child Protective Services agent, and other authorities to determine if the child will go home into family custody or stay at the detention center—this is known as "turning the corner." This girl has turned the corner: she has to stay at the facility, and she's miserable.

Ventura Youth Correctional Facility, Camarillo, California

Giddings State School, Giddings, Texas

The state of California spends $224,712 annually to house a juvenile in the new "green" Oakland facility. Oakland spent $4,945 on the education of a child in the Oakland public school system.

ABOVE: Rooms at District of Columbia's New Beginnings Youth Development Center in Laurel, Maryland, have chalkboard walls to allow inmates to draw on them. New Beginnings opened in May 2009 to replace Oak Hill Youth Center, also in Laurel.

OPPOSITE: Oak Hill Youth Center, Laurel, Maryland, closed in 2009

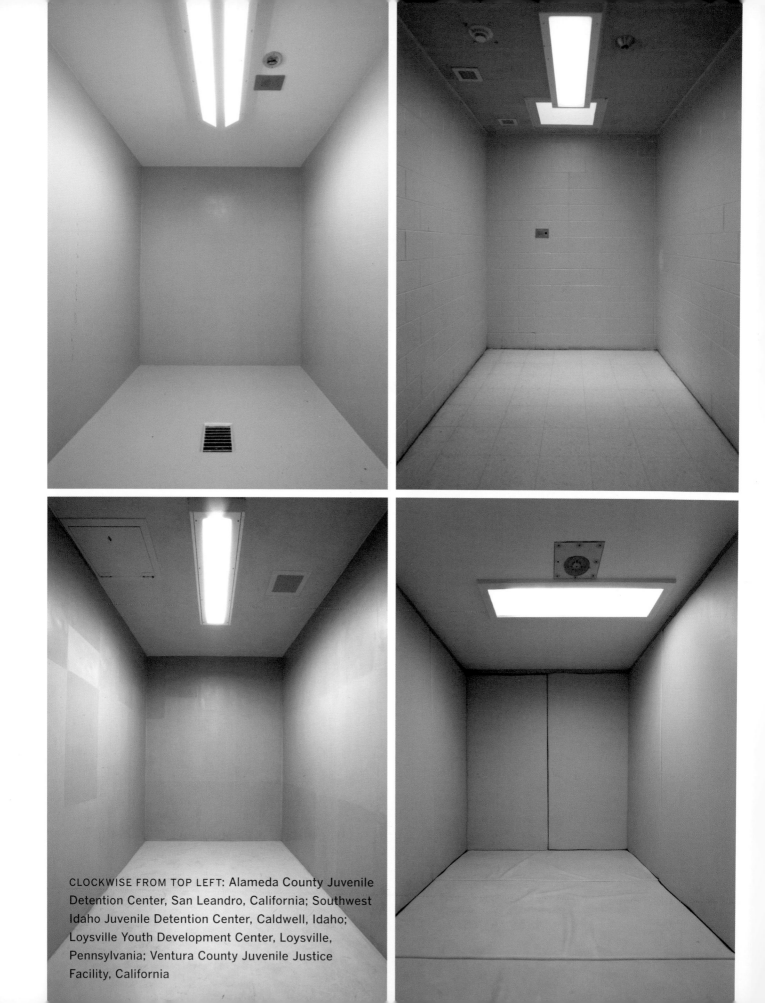

CLOCKWISE FROM TOP LEFT: Alameda County Juvenile Detention Center, San Leandro, California; Southwest Idaho Juvenile Detention Center, Caldwell, Idaho; Loysville Youth Development Center, Loysville, Pennsylvania; Ventura County Juvenile Justice Facility, California

"Time-out room" in the
educational wing of South Bend
Juvenile Correctional Facility,
South Bend, Indiana

ABOVE: The sweat lodge is a key element of the customs and religion of the Native American population. Juvenile detention facilities very rarely dedicate resources to accommodate this tradition.

MacLaren Youth Correctional Facility, Woodburn, Oregon, for boys aged 13–24

OPPOSITE: I'm from North Philly. My dad and nephews visit. He's a retired construction worker. I have no contact with my mom, who is on the streets. I been here 15 months, and I'm a platinum-plus level. I have this tattoo of Scarface with the words "Fuck You Pay Me" here [on his forearm]. I'm in for having 2 firearms. My 22-year-old sister got me into being a Muslim. I try to follow my religion but there are some things I can't do. Everybody is not perfect. —P. (Muslim name adopted), age 18

South Mountain Maximum Security in Pennsylvania, has a capacity of 90 young men; 95 percent of them are Muslim.

RIGHT: A juvenile plays ukulele during recreation time at Hawaii Youth Correctional Facility (HYCF), Kailua, Hawaii.

BELOW: Juveniles do yoga for exercise at Pima County Juvenile Detention Center, Tucson, Arizona.

LEFT AND BELOW: Bluett School in St. Louis, Missouri. The last resort school—for kids who have been thrown out of school for fighting, drugs, bad behavior, etc. The school can send them here and avoid court. The kids here have to attend smaller classes and after-school activities to keep them off the street.

125

At virtually every stage of the juvenile justice process, youth of color—Latinos and African Americans, particularly—receive harsher treatment than their white counterparts, even when they enter the justice system with identical charges and offending histories.

Twenty-three young men, undersupervised, at Orleans Parish Prison, Louisiana. There was a fight the night before, so staff has taken away privileges of TV, cards, and dominoes. The air conditioner is broken and it is August in New Orleans.

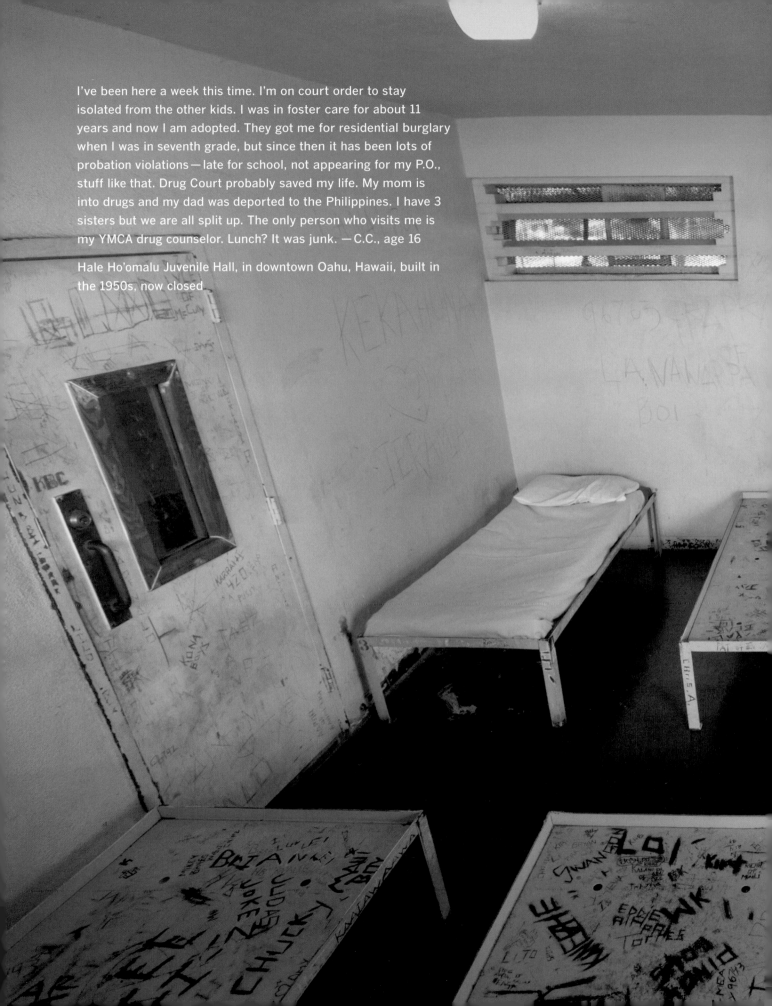

I've been here a week this time. I'm on court order to stay isolated from the other kids. I was in foster care for about 11 years and now I am adopted. They got me for residential burglary when I was in seventh grade, but since then it has been lots of probation violations—late for school, not appearing for my P.O., stuff like that. Drug Court probably saved my life. My mom is into drugs and my dad was deported to the Philippines. I have 3 sisters but we are all split up. The only person who visits me is my YMCA drug counselor. Lunch? It was junk. —C.C., age 16

Hale Ho'omalu Juvenile Hall, in downtown Oahu, Hawaii, built in the 1950s, now closed

ABOVE AND OPPOSITE: New juvenile detention facility in Oahu, Hawaii, designed to house 66 kids. Some administrators believe that the place is incorrectly built—that the architecture is wrong for treating and healing the kids. The design is essentially based on Pelican Bay, an adult maximum security facility in California. Kapolei, Oahu, Hawaii.

314

Racine Juvenile Detention, Racine, Wisconsin

Cook County Juvenile Detention Center in Chicago, Illinois. Each floor is one mile around. The basketball court gives a sense of the scale.

ABOVE: Mr. Brooks, a hearing officer, meeting with the boys about a fight earlier in the day at Cook County Juvenile Detention Center, Chicago, Illinois. They have been confined since the fight and can be held for a maximum of 36 hours in confinement.

OPPOSITE: I'm here on medical transition from Miller Camp. I was there 8 months. I'm in on 3 different second-degree robberies. My tats? I'm in the Fruit Town BRIMS (Black Revolutionary Independent Mafia Soldiers), part of the VNG (Van Ness Gangers). I want to go to Morehouse when I get out of here. —M.T., age 17

Central Juvenile Hall, Los Angeles, California

Black youth are 9 times as likely to be sentenced to adult prisons as white youth.

Male juvenile on a stationary bike in the gym area of
Racine Juvenile Detention, Racine, Wisconsin

Youth Offender System Facility, Pueblo, Colorado

CLOCKWISE FROM TOP LEFT: Ethan Allen School, Wales, Wisconsin; Central Juvenile Hall, Los Angeles, California; New Beginnings Youth Development Center, Washington, D.C.; Cook County Juvenile Detention Center, Chicago, Illinois. When queried about the food, one youth said, "Ain't going to be different from yesterday."

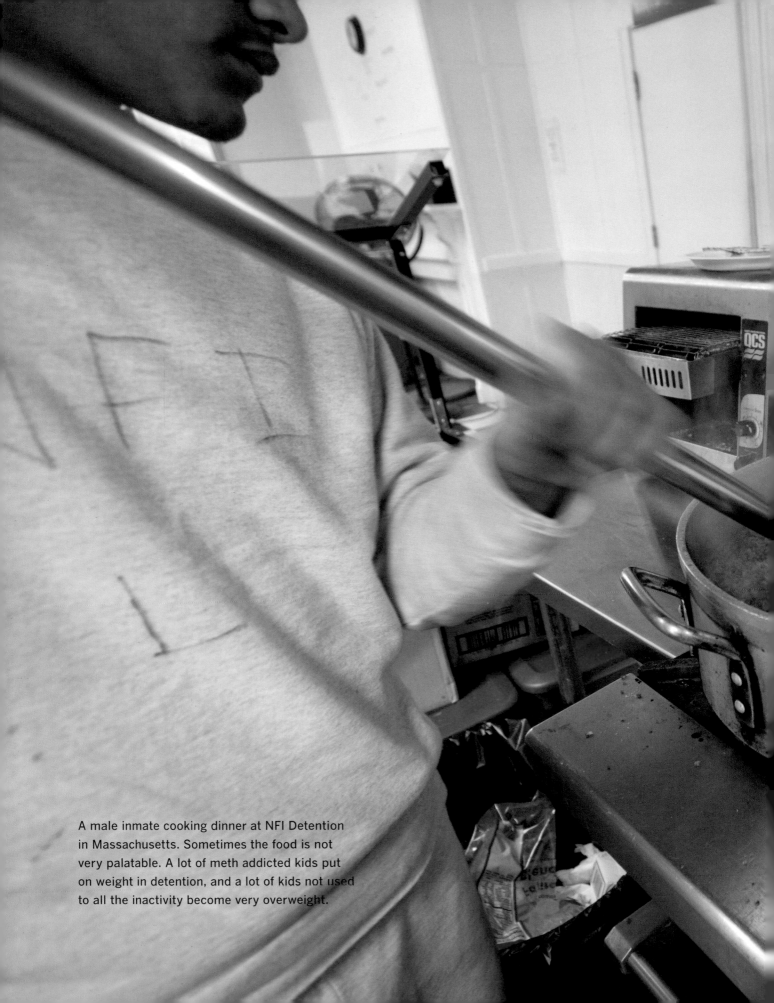

A male inmate cooking dinner at NFI Detention in Massachusetts. Sometimes the food is not very palatable. A lot of meth addicted kids put on weight in detention, and a lot of kids not used to all the inactivity become very overweight.

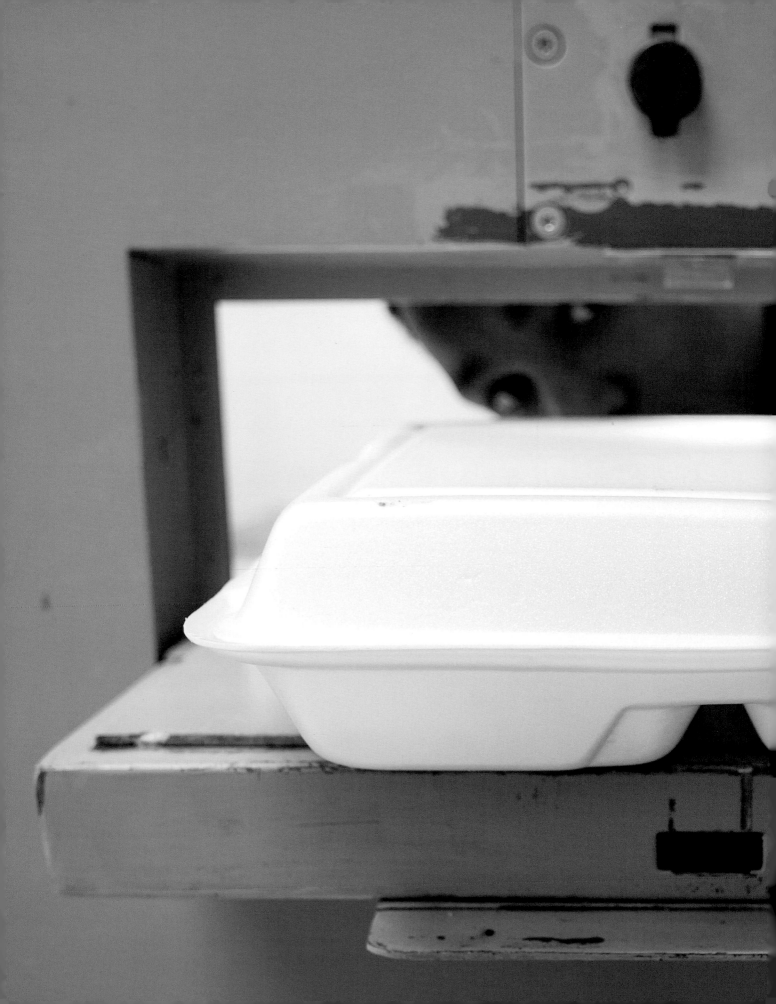

I'm doing my "seg time." I spend all day and all night in here. No mattress, no sheets, and I get all my meals through this slot. —J., age 16, in a segregation cell in South Bend Juvenile Correctional Facility, South Bend, Indiana

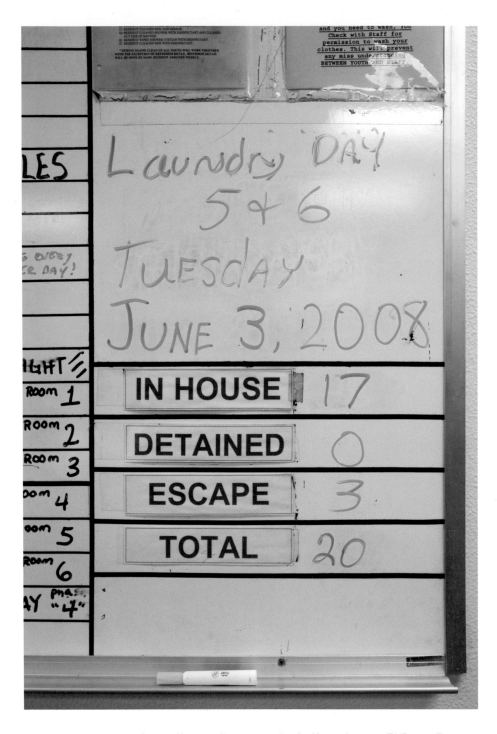

ABOVE: Whiteboard, Schaeffer medium security halfway house, El Paso, Texas

OPPOSITE: Sign at Oak Hill Youth Center, Laurel, Maryland, closed in 2009

150

NOTICE

THE FOLLOWING ITEMS ARE PROHIBITED IN THIS INSTITUTION

ILLEGAL DRUGS IE., MARIJUANA, COCAINE ETC.

PRESCRIPTION AND NON PRESCRIPTION DRUGS

TABLET OR LIQUID. MEDICINE CONTAINERS -

VIALS, BOTTLES AND PILL BOXES

EXPLOSIVE DEVICES - FIRECRACKERS, BULLETS

WEAPONS - FIREARMS, KNIVES, SHARP

INSTRUMENTS ETC.

ALCOHOLIC BEVERAGES - TOBACCO PRODUCTS.

MATCHES AND LIGHTERS.

I spent a year at TGK [Turner Guilford Knight Correction Center]. I was at the center for 9 days on charges of home invasion, kidnapping, armed carjacking, aggravated assault, battery, and armed battery. All the charges were dropped to juvenile. If the charges had been filed as adult, I could get 10 years' prison time. I'll probably serve 3 years — half of that if I behave well. In TGK, I was never able to touch my mom. After my first release from the center, she hugged me for the first time in over a year and we both cried and cried. All the visitation here is in the gym. It's set up for a hug with a parent and then you can sit holding hands. —S.M., age 15

Miami-Dade Regional Juvenile Detention
Center, Confinement Unit, Miami, Florida

I been here 8 months. Right now I'm reading *Metamorphosis* [by Franz Kafka]. I been in 20 or 25 fights here. I've got 2 counts of murder, rape, and assault. I stabbed my sister and her boyfriend and his friend. I beat their heads in with a cinder block and threw them in a pool. My sister lived. I spent some time in Citrus [mental hospital]. My brother was shot and bled to death in my arms. I blame all this on my father. He used to burn my hands and electrocute me, and he beat me with a baseball bat. I'll probably go to adult prison. Nobody visits me. —A.H., age 16

Miami-Dade Regional Juvenile Detention Center, Miami, Florida

The court says I got to be here 4 months. I'm here for burglary, and I got 10 open cases or more of past burglaries. I've been here 6 times, I think more. My parents don't live together. I never attended school outside the center. I went to a program called CAT [a youth outreach program] and spent 6 months in a moderate risk program. I have 3 brothers and a younger sister. Another sister died when she was very young. —A.N., age 18

Miami-Dade Regional Juvenile Detention Center, Miami, Florida

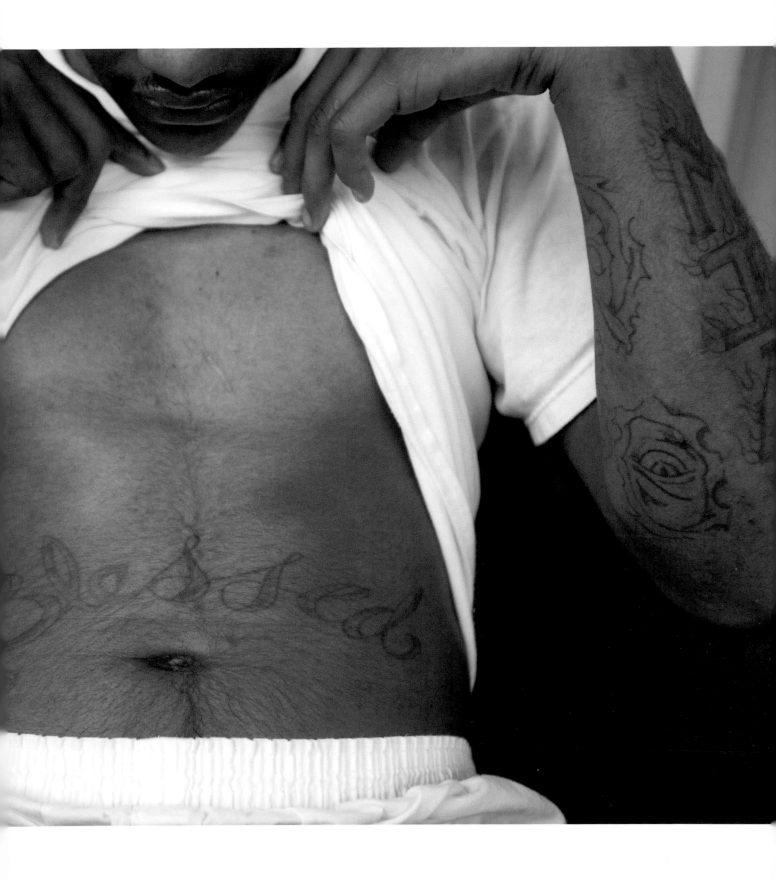

In most states, commitments to state custody are funded entirely with state funds, whereas local jurisdictions must foot the bill for community-based supervision and treatment programs.

Watkins Mill Park Camp, Lawson, Missouri, group meeting room

Boys Town Home, New York, a nonsecure boys detention facility with 12 beds. Youth are here for a few days to up to 6 months. The building is 4 stories tall with a yard and a basketball hoop. Everything is based on motivational behavioral modification: praise for simple positive actions. When you come into the room, every kid gets up and shakes your hand, tells you his name, and makes eye contact. The boys prepare meals together and eat together, along with the staff. At the table they learn and practice table manners.

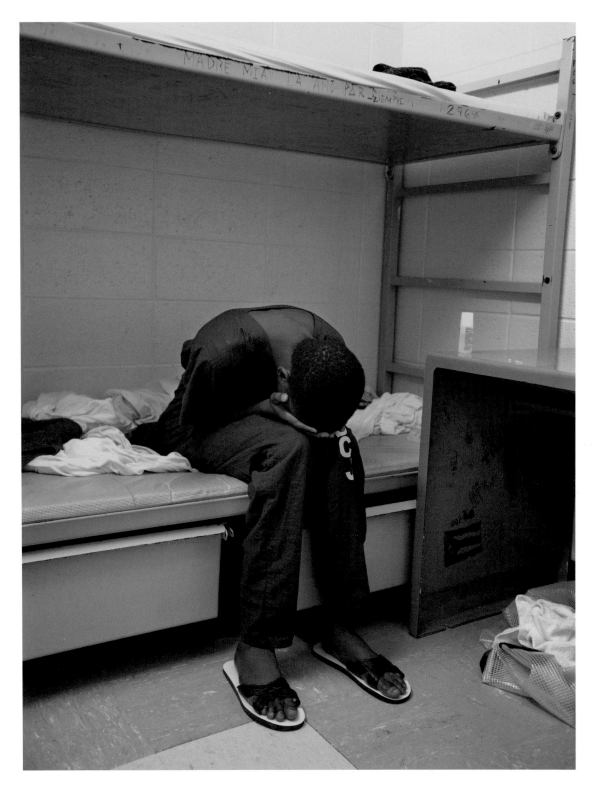

This is the first time I am here, ever. They are charging me with armed burglary of a residence. —K.T., age 16

Turner Guilford Knight (TGK) Correctional Center in Miami, Florida

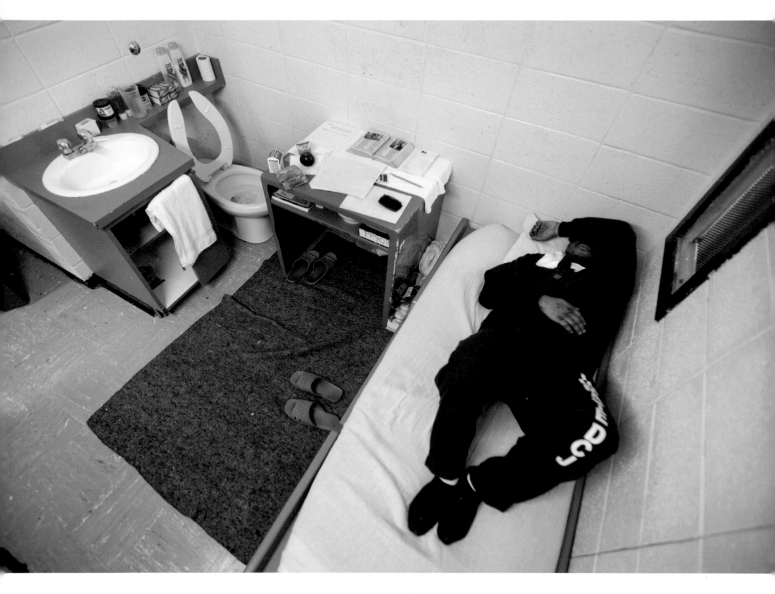

I been here for 3 years and 10 months and haven't been to trial yet. My mother tried to stab me and kill me when I was asleep so I ran out of the house. I'm here on 12 charges: 2 armed carjackings, armed robbery, armed burglary, 8 burglary, sexual battery, and gang charges. I don't blame nobody, I just made a mistake. I was 13. —R.F., age 17

Turner Guilford Knight Correctional Center, Miami, Florida

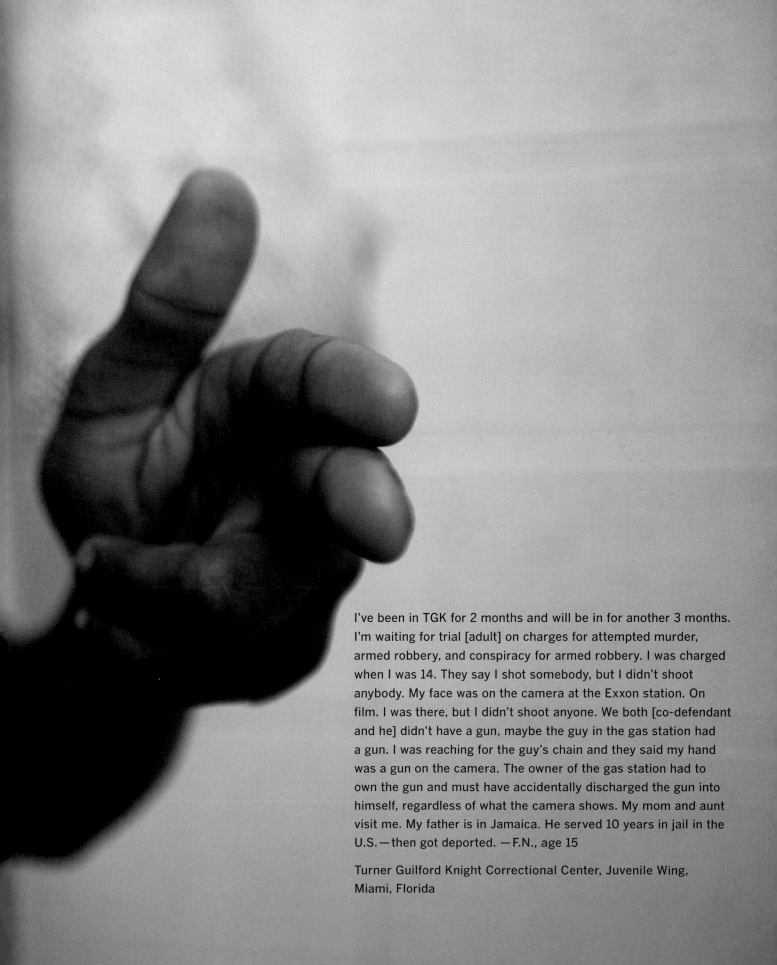

I've been in TGK for 2 months and will be in for another 3 months. I'm waiting for trial [adult] on charges for attempted murder, armed robbery, and conspiracy for armed robbery. I was charged when I was 14. They say I shot somebody, but I didn't shoot anybody. My face was on the camera at the Exxon station. On film. I was there, but I didn't shoot anyone. We both [co-defendant and he] didn't have a gun, maybe the guy in the gas station had a gun. I was reaching for the guy's chain and they said my hand was a gun on the camera. The owner of the gas station had to own the gun and must have accidentally discharged the gun into himself, regardless of what the camera shows. My mom and aunt visit me. My father is in Jamaica. He served 10 years in jail in the U.S.—then got deported. —F.N., age 15

Turner Guilford Knight Correctional Center, Juvenile Wing, Miami, Florida

ABOVE: I have been here 47 days. My parents and grandparents visit. My dad is a car salesman and my mom works at a glass place. I've been here before, but I am hoping this is my last time. —A.M., age 14

Southwest Idaho Juvenile Detention Center, Caldwell, Idaho

OPPOSITE: I hope I get out in March. Mostly depends on my level of achievement. We stuck in here today because one of the guys in our cottage didn't feel like getting out of bed, so we all stuck here. We have class here today too. I been here awhile but I want to go back to my home in north St. Louis. They let you wear your own clothes here. —B.D., age 16

Soaring Eagles Cottage in Hillsboro Treatment Center, Missouri

B.D. had his hand on his crotch under a sweatshirt. The director, Betty Dodson, said, "Take your hand off your imagination." He laughed and brought his hand up.

Control room at Racine Detention Facility,
Racine, Wisconsin

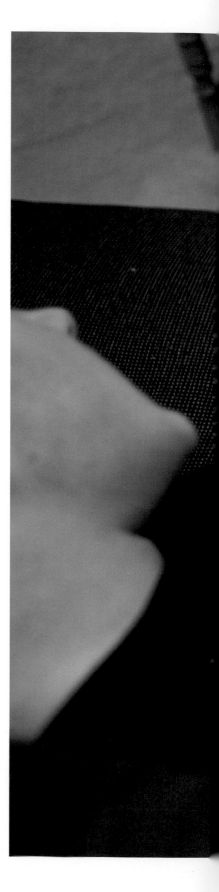

This is a time line of my offenses and my history. It sort of begins around age 7. I moved. Age 9, moved and Mom got married, then moved midway. Age 10, moved to Columbia. Age 11 met Dad, Dad goes to prison, moved to Boonville, got arrested. Age 12, started drugs, went to Boys & Girls Town, moved. Age 13, moved. Age 14, I got arrested, went to rehab, moved. Age 15, moved and got arrested. My mom is 8 months pregnant. I don't like her boyfriend. She's doing better now that she's sober. —D.J., age 16

Fulton Treatment Center in Fulton, Missouri

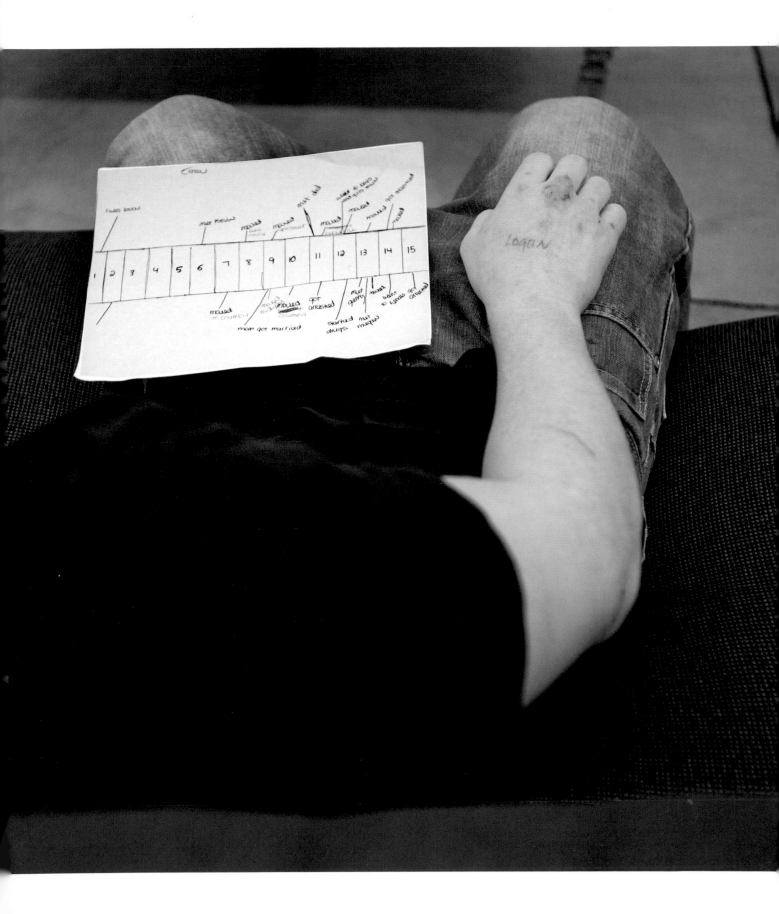

Probation hearing room at Ventura Youth Correctional Facility, Camarillo, California

Children as young as 11 have been sentenced to life without the possibility of parole.

I have 2 more days here, or less, then I go to an adult facility. I was convicted (with several co-defenders) of killing one of my friends' mother. I was 16, and it was a series of events—bad peer pressure and alcohol. The oldest of my friends—co-conspirators—was convicted on 4 counts. He was over 18 at the time so he was convicted as an adult. He has successfully appealed 3 of the convictions and had them overturned. He's waiting for the results of the last appeal. I'm the only one out of the 4 kids involved that received life without parole. I want to apply for clemency but can't find an attorney that would take it pro bono. I don't have the money for an appeal. I thought I might get 30 years to life but ended up with life without parole. I was convicted right after Measure 11 passed, from a small town where they wanted to set an example of how to punish juveniles. It appears that the Department of Corrections has become the Department of Punishment. We went to Canada and were at the border in a stolen car after we planned for about 4 or 5 hours how to kill the mother. We fled and were stopped at the Canadian side. I was brought back and interrogated by 2 male and 1 female detective from Oregon. I am not sure if I was Mirandized. There was no one that advocated for me in the room while I was being questioned. I have been here 7 years with DOC rather than OYA. I age out of here in 2 months and *hope* I go to Salem, where I might have the friendship and protection of Chris Cringle, who is somewhat notorious...look him up. I can either give up or try and do something with my life. I took a lot, so I am trying to give back by having received a paralegal degree through Blackstone. My biological mother and stepdad were a very bad crowd. My stepfather was a scummy street person. I've been given 2 life sentences. —S.P., age 24

MacLaren Youth Correctional Facility, Woodburn, Oregon

At the window is a treatment manager at SITP (Secure Intensive Treatment Program). "My evaluations don't mean anything in sentencing. I treat kids as they come in and while they are here—and have to say good-bye when many go on to the adult facility." The Supreme Court has ruled against life without parole for noncapital cases and is now taking up the issue of age and mitigating circumstances for juveniles in capital offenses.

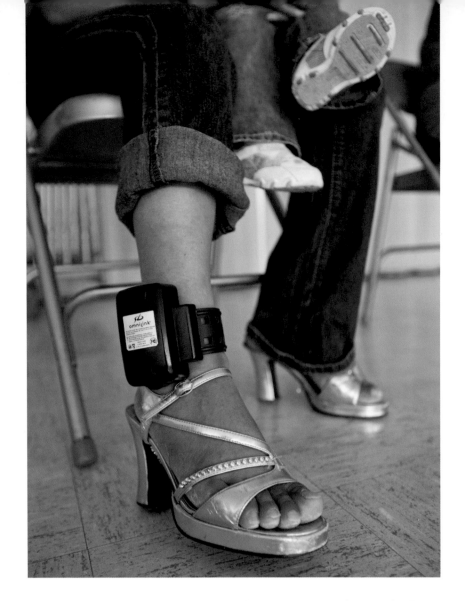

ABOVE: I was at the packing plant for about 16 months. I come here to St. Bridgette's for help. Father Paul does his best for us. ICE had a big raid, lots of trucks and men with guns and helicopters. They deported most of the people but kept some of us to go to court against the owners. They had a lot of minors working here. All of us were from the same little village in Guatemala. We live in houses that the company owns. I think they let me stay because of my baby. —R.T., age 16

Postville, Iowa

OPPOSITE: I have been running away my whole life. My parents divorced when I was 4. My father sexually abused me from age 5 to 9. My stepmother physically abused me. I was kidnapped by a pimp and prostituted out. I tried to run at one point and was shot in my butt. I was paralyzed for 2 weeks. I am a victim, according to my lawyers. I shouldn't be here. They are not charging me with anything, but they have set bail at $250,000. —R., age 16

Multnomah County Detention Facility, Multnomah County, Oregon

I have been here about 3 weeks. I got picked up for VOP. Not much to do here.
Mostly I write on the wall. I really don't want to talk to you. — A.W., age 16

Harrison County Juvenile Detention Center, Biloxi, Mississippi

"We have to recognize that incarceration of youth per se is toxic, so we need to reduce incarceration of young people to the very small dangerous few. And we've got to recognize that if we lock up a lot of kids, it's going to increase crime."

Dr. Barry Krisberg, the president of the National Council on Crime and Delinquency, faculty at the University of California, Berkeley

The "Wall of Shame," at Miami-Dade Regional Juvenile Detention Center, Miami, Florida: mug shots of kids that were released from the center and killed by gunshot wounds. "Expired" here indicates "deceased."

I live at home with my mother, 10-year-old brother, and stepfather. I don't know my real father. I hate school and have been suspended. I spend my time at home hanging with my friends. I have 2 older brothers and 1 older sister, all in their twenties, and they all don't live at home. I have been at King County for about a week and have been here 3 other times. They're thinking of moving up my charges to Robbery 1. I might be going to a decline status, not an auto decline, a person-on-person crime. I might be going to Residential Treatment Center to break the detention cycle…they tell me. —D.P., age 16

King County Juvenile Detention Center, Seattle, Washington

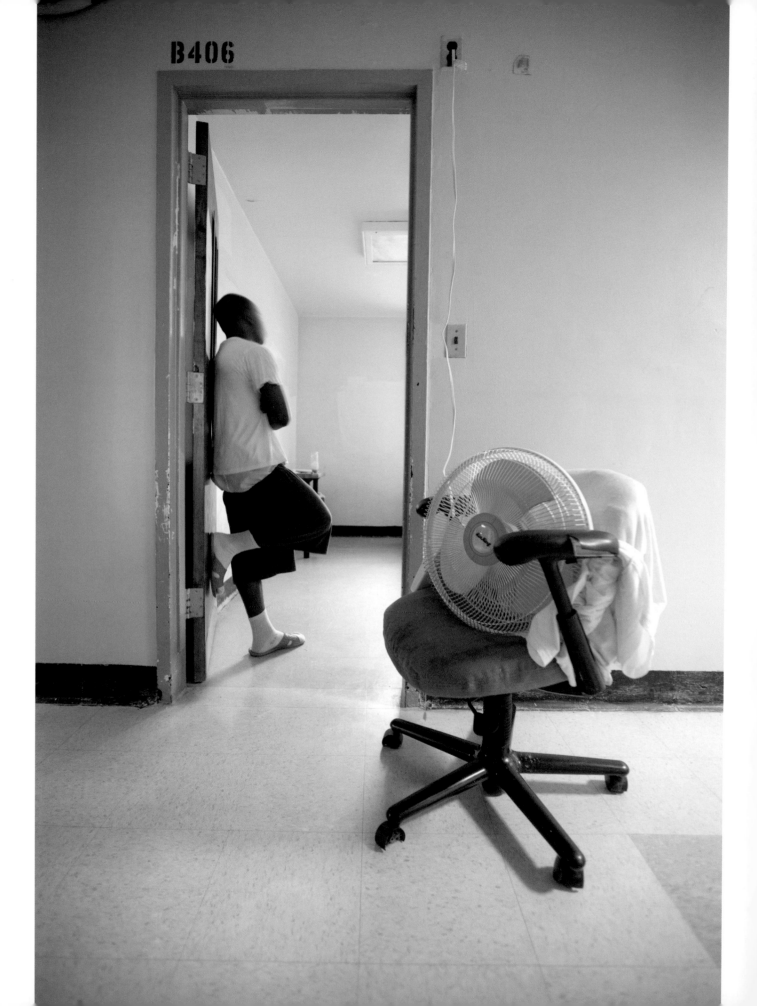

AFTERWORD by Richard Ross

"The study of art that does not result in making the strong
less willing to oppress the weak means little."
—Booker T. Washington, 1896

10 a.m. I am sitting in an intake cell with a fifth grader. He has just arrived. He is confused, worried, scared. He is barefoot and beltless. There is nothing in his concrete cell except a container of milk and a sandwich. He will be staying here until he is released to his mother at about 7 p.m. when she gets off work. She can't leave earlier for fear of losing her job. Every 10 minutes an officer checks on him. I try to comfort him by telling him his mommy will be here soon. He says he has gotten in trouble because he had a fight with another boy in his class.

3 p.m. Another state, another unit, another cell. Here the juvenile is a 17-year-old. He has been held since he was 13. Multiple charges, most violent. He has been held now almost 4 years without trial. He was "direct filed" as an adult, and his court-appointed attorney has been trying to get the charges dropped down to juvenile. The process takes time. The Sixth Amendment to the U.S. Constitution declares the right to a speedy trial by a jury of your peers. As an adult, almost 4 years might be contestable; juveniles have the least voice in this system. I try to call him but the counselor tells me, "They don't allow juveniles to use the phone, especially if you are not his attorney." I ask, "May I get the contact information for his attorney?" I am told, "He would have to give it to you and normally they can't use the phone and they are on lockdown anyway for an incident this weekend but he wasn't involved."

These are just a couple of brief anecdotes, stories of young lives reduced to a paragraph of information. What they have in common is poverty, violence, and a diminished view of the possibilities that the world can offer.

I've been locked up for 21 months. I haven't been sentenced yet. —D.P., age 16, Bridges Juvenile Center (Spofford), Bronx, New York, a secure detention facility built in 1957 with a maximum capacity of 75 kids, closed March 2011

At the outset of this project I wanted to give a voice to those with the least amount of authority in any U.S. confinement system. In 2006 I spoke with the juvenile prosecutor in El Paso, Texas, who had generously allowed me access to photograph. I inquired if he ever thought a system would be so successful at reformation that there would be no need for his position in the future. His response was daunting: "I will be here as long as the state of Texas keeps making 10-year-olds." Later I found 10-year-olds were not the youngest in the system. Nationwide the statutes were a checkerboard of rules, some mandatory, others discretionary, but many seemingly inappropriately applied.

This has been a difficult journey of learning about a world that is populated by administrators — a complex hierarchy of judges, staff, guards, families, and finally the juveniles. All the people in this chain, in one manner or another, had to agree to let me sit in a cell and allow me to listen to the story of the child. It has been a very long process.

After 5 years of working on this project I have visited more than 200 institutions in 31 states and spoken with more than 1,000 juveniles. There are well-meaning people in this system who are doing their best to change the lives of the juveniles in their care both inside and outside the institution. Some institutions and people were distrustful and wary, some self-critical, some proud and defensive. Regardless, gaining access was an ongoing negotiation until the last minute, when I was outside of the cell, talking to the juvenile and asking him or her for permission to enter his or her cell and world.

Quickly, I learned how to speak to children in detention and confinement. I learned to neutralize the authority of my age, height, and race by sitting on the floor and allowing the children to have control over the conversation. I always got a better response when they were either at eye-level or looking down at me. I had to learn skills and techniques to coax the histories and stories from those who spoke in the smallest of whispers. If and when I arrived at this position, I would sit on the concrete floor for 30 minutes or more, listening to stories of who visits, what they did during the day, how long they had been there, what the food, recreation, education, and people were like (no easy task after 1,000 interviews and with a bad back). They always had the option of saying, "Don't want to talk about that." And, on more than one occasion, they exercised it. But in most cases these young people were surprisingly candid and willing to open up and explain their world. At the end of the day I would leave the facility, call home, transcribe notes, and have a drink. These kids could not.

Portraying the presence of a human being—his or her demeanor, size, gender, race—without revealing his or her identity was daunting. A small tripod and small aperture allowed me to capture the architecture and have the faces blurred. I could bring only limited equipment—a camera, a tripod, a notepad, a curiosity, and a conscience.

During the making of this project I knew that disseminating the images I was producing would burn bridges in front of me. Since the work became public I have been giving license to the images, free of charge, to all facilities and advocates in the field.

This is a significant turn away from solely making a beautiful image and dealing with photographs as a commodity. Discovering the quote by Booker T. Washington that heads this afterword made a difference: "The study of art that does not result in the making of the strong less willing to oppress the weak means little." Not that all work has to have social significance, but I came to realize that there was another kind of beauty in doing work of this nature.

It may seem a cliché but in the end I felt I received more than I gave. Sitting on the floor of a cell and listening to a kid try to explain why his mother hasn't visited him in the 4 years he has been in prison is an odd gift to be given. Being engaged in the world, this world that, gratefully, I was able to visit rather than be born into, has been a rare opportunity.

ACKNOWLEDGMENTS

The children who populate this book and these institutions gave me access to their worlds and were willing to educate me. They were generous in their openness and their trust.

Many administrators and custodians of these lives opened up to me, in spite of the criticism they knew would be generated, with the faith that the work could lead to change and ultimately a better result for those entrusted in their care.

There is a significant group of administrators who care more for the protection of the institution than for the children and were determined to prevent any outsider from gaining entry. Fortunately, there is a majority who care enough for the juveniles to open their doors. The camera can be an unforgiving witness. It may capture a visual truth that does not allow explanation of a humane system administering care, treatment, and even love for these kids. Whereas some states barred their doors to scrutiny, there were others such as Missouri, Massachusetts, Colorado, Delaware, and Pennsylvania that not only allowed me in but made me feel welcome.

The project was assisted by support from Bart Lubow and Nel Andrews of the Annie E. Casey Foundation and their dedicated staff who graciously pushed me from being angry about conditions to learning how to advocate and effect change. The Guggenheim Foundation was instrumental in its support at the very earliest stage. The Center for Cultural Innovation assisted in supporting the development of a website and blog. The University of California, Santa Barbara, assisted with research grants and a platform from which to air my findings.

My studio manager Katy McCarthy always spoke of this project in a plural pronoun. It was a group effort, and Katy is defined by the word *indispensable*. When I took her to a shoot she cried as she took notes. She worked beyond the pain of these kids with a professionalism mixed with humanity that set a standard for me.

Assisting also in the seemingly endless data coordination and transmission were Sal Muñoz and Troy Small.

My great friend Laura Lindgren designed and managed production of the book with endless talent, support, and a healthy dose of reality.

My gratitude goes to Julien Robson, Stephen Foster, and Karen Sinsheimer, who are endlessly writing letters of recommendation for me, and to Gale Lewis, assistant public defender in Miami, Florida, for her generous assistance. Ian Kaplan helped open the first door.

Rick MacArthur at *Harper's Magazine* understood that the work was important and meaningful and he wanted to publish it and offered me as many pages as I needed. Stacey Clarkson at *Harper's* helped curate the work in a way that gave it full impact and allowed me a voice in that design.

The Nevada Museum of Art has supported this timely work by committing to an exhibition. The Wilhelm Hoppe Family Trust provided exclusive sponsorship for the exhibition. Ronald Feldman and Marco Nocello were always believers.

Several writers were willing to share their research: Jeff Goodale, Howard Savin, Deborah Smith Arthur, Bobbie Huskey, and Lindsay Hayes. Nancy Guerra and Kirk Williams shared their network in the academic worlds. Thanks go to the Juvenile Justice Information Exchange and its committed staff for disseminating the work online. Also noted are the assistance of Pete Brook of Prison Photography and Alan Moore of SMLXL.

Victor Rios and Cissy Ross, colleagues at UC Santa Barbara, helped me push this project from a book to an interdisciplinary class that we hope will aid in creating a group of young minds willing to act on the information we present.

Thank you, Cissy, Nick, and Leela, with all my heart and love. This work could never be done without the warmth, support, enthusiasm, and love of my family. After long days sitting on the floors of concrete cells and taking notes on the most heart-wrenching of autobiographies, I had a warm home and hearth to keep me sane. I wish any of the juveniles I dealt with had a small measure of this to keep them going.

NOTES

page 3: Office of Juvenile Justice and Delinquency Prevention *Statistical Briefing Book*. Released May 6, 2011, available online at http://www.ojjdp.gov/ojstatbb/court/qa06201.asp?qaDate=2008; Charles Puzzanchera, Benjamin Adams, and Melissa Sickmund, *Juvenile Court Statistics 2006–2007*. Pittsburgh, PA: National Center for Juvenile Justice, 2010.

page 5: Melissa Sickmund, T. J. Sladky, Wei Kang, and Charles Puzzanchera, "Easy Access to the Census of Juveniles in Residential Placement" (2011). Available online at http://www.ojjdp.gov/ojstatbb/ezacjrp/.

page 7: Neal Hazel, "Cross-National Comparison of Youth Justice," London: Youth Justice Board, 2008.

page 9: American Correctional Association, as cited in Amanda Petteruti, Nastassia Walsh, and Tracy Velazquez, "The Costs of Confinement: Why Good Juvenile Justice Policies Make Good Fiscal Sense," Justice Policy Institute, 2009.

page 21: interview with the author.

page 35: Sickmund et al, "Easy Access to the Census of Juveniles in Residential Placement."

page 43: Thomas A. Loughran, Edward P. Mulvey, Carol A. Schubert, Jeffrey Fagan, Alex R. Piquero, and Sandra H. Losoya, "Estimating a Dose-Response Relationship Between Length of Stay and Future Recidivism in Serious Juvenile Offenders," *Criminology* 47, no. 3 (2009).

page 51: Sandy Cullen, "Lawsuit Filed by Parents of Grant County Boy Accused of Sex Assault," *Wisconsin State Journal* 10:20, www.madison.com, November 17, 2011.

page 57: Mark W. Lipsey, "The Primary Factors that Characterize Effective Interventions with Juvenile Offenders: A Meta-Analytic Overview," *Victims and Offenders* 4, no. 2 (2009).

page 67: "No Place for Kids," Annie E. Casey Foundation report, 2011.

page 77: "No Place for Kids."

page 85: "Jailing Juveniles: The Dangers of Incarcerating Youth in Adult Jails in America," Campaign for Youth Justice report, 2007.

page 97: Richard A. Mendel's calculations for the Annie E. Casey Foundation using data from the Survey of Youth in Residential Placement online database, available at https://www.dataxplorer.com/Project/ProjUser/AdhocTableType.aspx?reset=true&ScreenID=40.

page 109: California Department of Corrections and Rehabilitation, "Safety and Welfare Plan: Implementing Reform in California," March 31, 2006.

page 114: top row to bottom row, left to right: New Orleans Youth Study Center, Juvenile Detention Facility, New Orleans, Louisiana; Ventura County Juvenile Justice Facility, Ventura, California; Santa Barbara County Juvenile Hall, Santa Barbara, California; King County Youth Service Center, Seattle, Washington; Southwest Idaho Juvenile Detention Center, Caldwell, Idaho; Southwest Idaho Juvenile Detention Center, Caldwell, Idaho; Summit View Facility, Las Vegas, Nevada; Ventura County Juvenile Justice Facility, Ventura, California; Nevada Youth Training Center, Elko, Nevada; Salt Lake Valley Detention Center, Salt Lake City, Utah; King County Youth Service Center, Seattle, Washington; Metro Regional Youth Detention Center, Atlanta, Georgia.

page 115: top row to bottom row, left to right: Salt Lake Valley Detention Center, Salt Lake City, Utah; Highland Residential Center, Highland, New York; Mendota Juvenile Treatment Center, Mendota, Wisconsin; Summit View Facility, Las Vegas, Nevada; Harris County Psychiatric Center Juvenile Detention Wing, Houston, Texas; Rader Juvenile Detention Center, Sand Springs, Oklahoma; Santa Cruz County Juvenile Hall, Fenton, California; Rader Juvenile Detention Center, Sand Springs, Oklahoma; King County Youth Service Center, Seattle, Washington; Metro Regional Youth Detention Center, Atlanta, Georgia; Juvenile Detention Facility, Greenville, Mississippi; Metro Regional Youth Detention Center, Atlanta, Georgia.

page 117: H. D. Palmer, deputy director for external affairs, California Department of Finance.

page 127: "And Justice for Some: Differential Treatment of Youth of Color in the Justice System," National Council on Crime and Delinquency, January 2007, downloaded from www.nccdcrc.org/nccd/pubs/2007jan_justice_for_some.pdf.

page 141: "And Justice for Some: Differential Treatment of Youth of Color in the Justice System."

page 173: http://www.amnesty.org/en/news-and-updates/13-year-old-us-boys-murder-trial-could-violate-international-law-2011-01-24.

pages 157, 181: "No Place for Kids."